ALCHE
OF THE
SOUL

*The Eros and Psyche Myth
as a Guide to Transformation*

MARTIN LOWENTHAL

NICOLAS-HAYS, INC.
Lake Worth, FL

First published in 2004 by
Nicolas-Hays, Inc.
P. O. Box 540206
Lake Worth, FL 33454-0206
www.nicolashays.com

Distributed to the trade by
Red Wheel/Weiser, LLC
65 Parker St. • Ste. 7
Newburyport, MA 01950
www.redwheelweiser.com

Library of Congress Cataloging-in-Publication Data

Lowenthal, Martin.
   Alchemy of the soul : the Eros and Psyche myth as a guide to transformation /
   Martin Lowenthal.-- 1st American pbk. ed.
      p. cm.
   Includes bibliographical references and index.
   ISBN 0-89254-096-6 (pbk. : alk. paper) 1. Spiritual life. 2. Self-actualization
   (Psychology)--Religious aspects. 3. Apuleius. Psyche et Cupido. 4. Alchemy--
   Religious aspects. I. Title.
BL624.L672 2004
204'.4--dc22   2004017923

Cover design by Phillip Augusta. Text design by Kathryn Sky-Peck.
Typeset in 10 Sabon

PRINTED IN THE UNITED STATES OF AMERICA

The paper used in this publication meets the minimum requirements of the
American National Standard for Information Sciences—Permanence of Paper for
Printed Library Materials Z39.48–1992 (R1997).

CONTENTS

APPENDIX

ACKNOWLEDGMENTS

I AM GRATEFUL TO Robert Bly and Gioia Timpanelli. Their tireless dedication to working with the deeper significance of great stories and their encouragement of the creative process grounded in both tradition and personal experience has led to much of my own writing and teaching with stories. I have worked with and been worked by the myth of Eros and Psyche since 1964, and it was after meeting Robert and Gioia in the early 1980's that I created a two-day workshop on this story as a guide to psycho-spiritual development.

I owe special gratitude to Martín Prechtel who inspired me to write this book through our conversations over the years about sacred stories, his teachings, and his own wonderful book *Disobedience of the Daughter of the Sun*.

In my retelling of the story of Eros and Psyche, I have drawn on a number of translations: H. E. Butler, *The Metamorphoses or Golden Ass of Apuleius of Madaura*, Clarendon Press, 1910; Robert Graves, *The Golden Ass of Apuleius*, Pocket Library, 1954; and E. J. Kenney, *Apuleius: Cupid and Psyche* and *The Golden Ass: A New Translation*, Cambridge University Press, 1990 and Penguin Books, 1998, respectively. I have also been guided by my own reading of the Latin.

I want to thank Jerome Petiprin for his commentary and feedback on the early version of the manuscript. I am also deeply grateful to my wife, Karen Edwards, for her support during my writing and her help in editing the first draft of this book. And great gratitude to my publisher, Nicolas-Hays, for assistance and thoughtful work throughout the process of bringing this book to the public.

My gratitude and love for all my teachers exceed any expression I could make here. May this effort be a worthy carrier of their great gifts and a small contribution to their legacy. May this book be of benefit to all those who read it and may it serve to honor the magnificence and enrich the life of this timeless story.

INTRODUCTION

HOW MANY OF US STRUGGLE WITH THE forces of love,
fear, doubt, loss, grief, and longing in our efforts to live more completely? We go through life seeking to feel as if we belong, and hoping to experience a sense of home in the world. We often feel that,
if only we can find our true love (while somehow avoiding the
oceanic feelings and forces that terrify us), we will in some way
solve the central problem of our lives: how to heal from the
wounds of living and feel whole again.

Too often, we avoid the tensions of love and fear, of grief and
anger, of passion and security by settling into comfortable routines
and diminished dreams, only occasionally glimpsing a sense of
enthusiastic, body-tingling, out-loud, foot-stomping, joyfully
painful aliveness. We mistake the loving nature of the universe for
a cuddly, warm embrace, forgetting that it is more truly embodied
in the ferocious challenges that compel us to grow beyond ourselves into the world of nature, of relationships and community,
and of the beautifully uncompromising sacred dimensions of life.
We curse these challenges, until we finally realize that they represent opportunities to develop resourcefulness and strength so we
can reach for another level of aliveness. They force us to undertake
the uncomfortable and uninvited task of making something exquisitely beautiful of our lives. How much better our lives would be if
we could just accept their invitation to generate new life, not just
for our own benefit, but for that of others and the invisible world
of the sacred.

The myth of Eros and Psyche depicts how all these passions, forces, challenges, tensions, and opportunities make up the fabric of an authentic life. It grounds us in the knowledge that they arise in the lives of all humans in some form. When we insulate ourselves from all these dynamics of real life and live in a world of fantasy and comfort, we fail to live out the lesson of the story and fulfill the potential encoded in us as human beings. Buddha identified the reality of suffering as a great noble truth. Our challenge is to create fruitful meaning and beauty from that suffering, rather than perpetuating and enlarging it into more suffering.

In our fragmented world, time is segmented, knowledge is divided into academic fiefdoms, communities are dispersed and temporary, and culture is reduced to lifestyle without the depth of wisdom. In this world, the heart of the sacred and the richness of collective creation and participation are divorced from daily meaning and activities by an overwhelming secular materialism, by numbing entertainment, by polarized thinking about morals and religion, gender and sexuality, politics and class, and by pervasive self-preoccupation. All this fragmentation calls out for a revitalization of the teachings that embrace a rich, full, and integrated life.

The price of the new vitality we seek has always been the same. The price is ourselves. We make payment through our dedication to our own transformation and to being a beneficial presence in our families, our communities, our society, our world, and our planet. No lesser payment will do. Nor can we accomplish our goal through mere exposure to profound ideas or by treating these ideas as interesting entertainment.

In modern, secular, scientific culture, the high priests of a literalist empiricism and disinterested rationality have declared that myth, storytelling, and alchemy are simply forms of sloppy thinking and imaginative hallucination. A smaller, yet powerful, cultural movement of literalist, religious fundamentalists has also attacked the classic myths and transformation teachings as heretical and false inspirations of the devil that challenge church dogma. As a culture, we have allowed these narrow fundamentalists—both secular and religious—to hijack the great mythological teachings that provide the stage upon which the drama of our religious life is played out.

We must reclaim our sacred birthright to the spiritual teachings of the past and revitalize them with love and wisdom, just as Psyche, revived by Eros, claimed a place in heaven. The life of these stories must be renewed with vision and life energy so that it can continue its heroic work for our benefit, individually and collectively, now and in the future.

Myth invites you not only to relate to these stories, but to invest them with your own meanings. The retelling of sacred stories and their subsequent interpretation invites you to bring to the tale your own ideas of significance, your truths, and your contributions to the legacy of the myth through generations. By becoming an active carrier of myths and their teachings, you, in your own unique way, keep the myth alive for the benefit of yourself and future generations—indeed, for all the guests in this rich and troubled world. May my own retelling of the tale be of benefit to you and to all who are touched directly or indirectly by this humble book.

PART ONE

The Power of Myth

Chapter One

ANCIENT ROOTS, SACRED MESSAGE

At first Chaos was, and Night, and dark Erebus, and wide Tartarus;
there was no earth, nor air, nor heaven; but first of all black-winged
Night laid a wind-egg in the boundless bosom of Erebus, from
which in revolving time sprang the much-desired Eros, his back glit-
tering with golden wings, like the swift whirlwinds.

ARISTOPHANES

The ancient roots and sacred message of the story of Eros and Psyche come to the surface through an examination of much older Greek images of Eros that center around the creation of the universe and the origination of differentiation from a primal unity. In the ancient texts, Eros was *androgyne*, having the qualities of both genders and thus containing the potential for generating all phenomena. These early stories were part of the mythological heritage that resonated with informed listeners and practitioners of the mystery schools at the time.

The cultural and spiritual atmosphere out of which the original myth grew plays an essential part in the shaping of the story. In this spiritual landscape, in a realm beyond time and causality (for the true beginning is not to be found in the cosmos), distinct impressions appear as the First Cause, even though, in time, each seems to contain within itself a still prior condition.[1] Each moment, cycle, and era arises from the residue of the prior time, its blossoms withering and providing the ground for something new. Yet the new is really the old that has defied dissolution—perhaps a residue of some prior universe.

The making of the myth of Eros and Psyche begins at some level in original Chaos—primordial, formless matter in formless space. Beyond qualities, Chaos exists eternally and uncreated, boundlessly vast, as pure openness. It is neither dark nor light, moist nor dry, hot nor cold, but all things together and undifferentiated.

From original Chaos came Great Night (Nox) and Darkness (Erebus). This sister and brother and their parent, not realizing they were all family, ignored each other for aeons. Being boundless and not bonded to or by anything, each believed itself to be everything.

Whether out of an excess of being or some sudden impulse, Great Night felt stirrings. She sensed the movement filling her body, if you can call it a body. The movement was wind. The motility of wind excited her and she felt something emerging from her body. Until then, she had not realized that she even had the potential for differentiation, for manifesting anything less than her whole being.

Suddenly, Night planted a spirit-egg in the bosom of Darkness/Silence. In the time before time, in the cycle that preceded cycles, Eros, whom some call Phanes, was hatched from this egg, emerging double-sexed, four-headed, and golden-winged. Through his birth, he set the universe in motion.

Eros (the primordial love god) as Phanes ("revealer") created Earth, sky, Heaven, Sun, and Moon. Great Night also named him Ericepaius ("feeder on heather"), a buzzing celestial bee, carrier and dispenser of the nectar of divinity. From Eros issued all the gods and goddesses. The very act of creation was an act of love. The vibration of love echoed through all existence as relationship—relationship to the primal parent, relationship of siblings, and relationship of lovers as they mated and expanded the universe and web of creation. Every one of them carried a seed, a genetic pattern of Eros, that connected them to each other and to their original source, and this seed was passed on to their issue.

So the union of indeterminate Night (the formless capacity to take form) and pervasive Darkness (the formative power) gave rise to Eros, from whom all else was created, by whom all things are related, and through whom all relationships derive their attraction and their bonding quality. In turn, from relationship arose time and place. Indeed, all form issued from this phenomenon of Eros.

Eros brought desire to the universe. Before Eros established desire as a base for relating and creating, however, the seed of desire must have been latent in all that gave rise to Eros. Or perhaps everything arose simultaneously. In fact, the logic of sequence in time may not apply to these dimensions, which are beyond our mental understanding and verbal description.

Great Night also named golden-winged Eros Protogenus Phaëthon ("first-born shiner"), the primal radiance or luminosity represented by the sun. Eros' four heads correspond to the symbolic animals of the four seasons: the ram (Zeus/spring), the lion (Helius/summer), the serpent (Hades/winter), and the bull (Dionysus/new year).

Under the influence of Eros, the formless, the formative, and form itself came to know each other and distinctions appeared. Forms had to arise from the primal state of being, because a frame was needed to see and hear and touch any and all of the potential qualities implicit in the formless state, in pure being.

The heat of Eros ignited the furnace in the universe and the hearths in all the smaller universes. This heat is at once cosmic and innermost. It is the charged atmosphere we breathe and in which we move. It is the warm breath we bring forth from the core of our body and pass to the world.

With Eros came existence and Reality, a dimension of being that must have always been there, but only now became evident. Reality gave rise to concepts like "now" and "here," and from Reality issued Presence.

Reality resembles a globe one half of which is land and the other water. The land always surrounds the water, making it a lake, and the water surrounds the land, making it an island. The paradoxical nature of Reality—as boundless and bound, totally open and totally manifest, empty and filled by Presence, terminal and eternal—lies hidden within all that flowed from that primal creation.

Until the arrival of Eros, each quality in the universe did not even know whether it existed or not. As distinctions became manifest, the gods thought: "If this relates to that yet is not that, and that relates to all these other things, then the entire universe must be my relations, my family." Each knowing contained the thought that it was the world. Yet it was still a world without meaning. So Eros—known as Phanes, Ericepaius, Protogenus Phaëthon, Zeus, Amor, and later as Cupid—took on many additional qualities that gave order to the chaos and significance to form.

The reverberations of love, relationship, desire, and passion gave rise to all that troubles all beings, gods included, and all that radiates with beauty. Suddenly, certainty and uncertainty arose to compete for the minds of all who seek to live a meaningful life. For with creation came time, and with time, causality and death. Whatever has a beginning in time has an end in time. Every child of Eros is haunted by this impending end. Each of us thinks: "If only I could harness the great powers of Eros, this enemy could be conquered."

With the creation of causal relationships, time arose, and with time, death emerged to keep the cycles going and give new possibilities a chance. But if all things die, what is beyond deterioration? What is immortal? The openness from which love arose, the relationships of things as manifestations of that primal love, the fullness of space to include all that arises, including tensions and conflicts, and the cycle of their birth and death and rebirth—these do not change and are not subject to the temporal world.

Those who came to realize that death was a blessing saw that it made further creation possible and reminded them that all they could count on was open Presence. These enlightened ones found the key to eternity beyond time and to freedom in their original nature. These realized beings became the gods, while those who could not transcend the haunting sense of death remained in the shadow of eternity.

These haunted ones must have felt that Eros had a mischievous and wicked nature to have given them death along with life—a life, moreover, aggravated by an awareness of death. This is our dilemma as human beings seeking to make our way in a paradoxical world filled with the love that makes life possible, and the treacherous dangers that surround us all the time.

With the emergence of time and space, of gods, of Heaven and Earth, of water and air and fire, things took on shapes and stories. There were endless shapes and countless stories, many of them variations on the same subject. Gods overlapped and merged and swapped places, but always within the frame of the fundamental relationships that had been laid out in the original design of the universe. Indeed, the names and stories of the gods change with the times—father becomes son, mother becomes daughter, daughter becomes mother, sister becomes wife, and brother becomes husband. The fact that the gods simply exist beyond time does not make them invulnerable. They are subject to the same cycles and reformations that afflict any species born on Earth that evolves and must regenerate. For the gods, this occurs in the ebb and flow of consciousness.

With time, the gods and goddesses needed to assert their own autonomy and primacy. As they recognized the spark of Eros in themselves, they conceived that they had created it and could cultivate it in their own ways. So double-sexed Eros, the father/mother, was first split into father Eros and mother Aphrodite/Isis. In later times, Eros became the son, the child to be raised by Zeus, Aphrodite, and Hephaestus. And as the works of creation expanded, as Heaven and Earth arose, as all the elements and all creatures, all the vast universes and all the small universes came into being, each carried this flame of Eros, this unstoppable impulse to generate and to relate. And each was a parent of this fire and a weaver of the nets of connections, developing its potential in its own way, thereby infinitely elaborating the possibilities of manifestation and the threads of connection.

Eros as father/son and Aphrodite as mother/daughter wove between all creation—gods, elements, seasons, worlds, creatures, and humans—threads of emotion, desire, and connection that hold together the fabric of relationships for the universe.

The myth of Eros and Psyche is one of many stories about the same gods and goddesses, all seeking to reveal something of the deeper nature of the relationships and dynamics that guide us in our own journey through the everlasting cycles. It portrays our service to the sacred qualities that make our efforts worthy. The truth that resides in every moment and is pointed to in every authentic sacred gesture hides beneath the surface of each part of this tale. Listen carefully as it unfolds and release all your assumptions about heroes, villains, and victims.

In the time of our story, Aphrodite plays the role of a great goddess who can and does govern birth, life, love, death, time, and fate. She is the force that reconciles humans to all forces through the senses, wisdom, and sexual mysticism. The Greek Aphrodite, who was worshipped in Egypt as Isis, in Sumeria as Inanna, in Babylonia as Ishtar, in the Near East as Ashtoreth, and was known in Roman times as Venus, reveals the mysteries of the gods, of life, of death, and of spiritual realization. Invoking her name gives life. Under her direction, disciples realize great bliss and achieve immortality.

When did all this happen? Is it still happening? A moment ago, or now, or in a future aeon? Is it always happening, again and again, because it is the nature of being, of life, and of the sacred context in which we live? And what was it that hosted and witnessed all these arisings? Whose eye caught all these things in the net of its sight and gathered them so we could speak of them and be nourished by their flesh? The answers to these and other questions will emerge as we explore the myth itself.

8

Chapter 2

EROS AND PSYCHE

The glory of God is man fully alive.

SAINT IRANEAUS

Our story,[1] which began in the stirrings before time, now begins anew in time on Earth in a certain city where a king and queen had three daughters, all quite pleasing to the eye. While the beauty and charms of the two eldest were praised, words, gestures, and music could not be found adequate to describe the awe-inspiring beauty and wondrous qualities of the youngest daughter, Psyche. It was rumored that Psyche had been born when a dewdrop from Heaven fell upon the land.[2]

So great was Psyche's beauty that people from far and wide came to gaze upon her. They marveled at her and claimed her as the great goddess, Aphrodite, sprung from the depth of the sea and born of a foamy wave. Or perhaps Heaven had rained a fresh procreative dew and the Earth, not the sea, had given birth to a second Aphrodite in all the splendor of flowering maidenhood.

Psyche's fame increased daily. Mortals flocked to see the wonder and glory of the maid, abandoning the temples of Aphrodite, leaving her rites undone, her altars in disrepair and soiled, her contributions disregarded, her images uncrowned, and her ceremonies neglected. Their hearts and minds, captivated by the mortal beauty of the young girl, left the true power of the great goddess untapped and disrespected. Young Psyche was greeted on her morning walks with food and flower offerings, as if she contained within her person the energies, wisdom, and power of the goddess.

Aphrodite herself grew angry with the divine honors and worship bestowed on Psyche. With divine rage, she said to no one in particular: "For the sake of Heaven, whoever thought I would be treated like this? I, Aphrodite, the source of all the elements, the womb of created things, the loving mother of all the world, am I expected to share my sovereignty and place with a pretentious mortal maid while my name is reduced from its heavenly height? Am I to be content with the reflected glory of the worship paid to this imposter? Shall a girl that is fated for death parade in my stead, receiving the attention that was meant for timeless beings? Was it in vain that the shepherd, Paris, with the approval of Zeus, chose me above other goddesses for my beauty and splendor? No! No! No! This is absurd! I cannot let this silly, naïve, and confused creature, whoever she may be, usurp my glory any longer. Soon enough she will be sorry for her fine looks and sick at heart for the beauty that will be her curse."

Aphrodite immediately called her winged son, Eros—that untamed youth feared in Heaven and on Earth, who, armed with arrows and torch aflame, knowing no boundaries and holding no respect for the rules, infects all with unquenchable desires. Knowing his inclination for mischief and sport, she drew him to the city where Psyche lived and told him the whole story of the misguided cult that had grown up around her. Groaning with indignation, she entreated: "I implore you, darling, by all the bonds of love that bind you to me who bore you, use the sweet wounds of your arrows and the honeyed burns of your fires to afflict this pretentious and feckless beauty. If you have any respect for me, you will set this right. This one thing I would have you do with unfaltering determination. See that the maiden falls desperately in love with some perfect outcast—someone with no health, rank, or fortune, someone so wounded that there is none in the world to rival his misery."

Having spoken, she kissed him long and fervently with parted lips. Then she, like the flowing of the tide, returned to her original home of the sea where the waves calmed at the touch of her rosy feet. The very depths greeted her and the sea gods did her bidding as if given instructions ahead of time. The daughters of Nereus sang in harmony. Poseidon with bristling blue-green beard, came with his wife, Amphitrite, and their son, Palaemon, riding a dolphin. From far and wide came hosts of Tritons, one blowing softly on his conch-shell, another protecting Aphrodite from the heat of the sun with a silken parasol, a third holding a mirror before her mistress's eyes, while others, harnessed to her carriage, carried her onward. Such was the host that escorted Aphrodite as she traveled to the halls of the ocean.

Over time, Psyche found no real satisfaction in all the honors paid her and began to rue her loveliness. Everyone gazed at her from a distance; no king, prince, or commoner ever came forward and dared to make love to her. All wondered at her beauty as they would an exquisite statue. Both of her less beautiful sisters were courted and married to kings, but Psyche remained unwed. Her body grew ill and her spirit broken. She hated her loneliness and her solitude, loathing in her heart the beauty that charmed so many.

Her father was beset by great grief for his daughter and a fear that the gods might be angry that his subjects had made so much of her, since drought had befallen the land. He decided to consult the ancient oracle of Apollo at Miletus. He offered the customary prayers and burnt offerings, and asked where he could find a husband for his daughter, whom nobody would marry.

Apollo delivered his oracle:

On a high mountain's craggy summit, place the maid
In funeral wedlock robes arrayed.
Hope not for a bridegroom born of mortal seed,
For he is of a mischievous, wild, and fierce dragon breed
Who flies all-conquering on airy wing,
With fire and sword he makes his harvesting;
Great Zeus himself holds him in dread,
And his power quakes the darksome river of the dead.

The once-happy king returned home in distress and immediately told his queen of Psyche's ordained fate as spoken by the oracle. They brooded and wept for several days. As time passed, they knew the cruel command had to be obeyed.

The dreaded wedding day arrived. Psyche donned robes more fitting a funeral than a joyous event. The processional torches burned with a sooty and sputtering flame. Instead of a happy wedding march, the flutes played a mournful lament. The marriage chorus howled with grief more than song. The poor bride wiped her own tears with the bridal veil, meant to hide the fearsome joy of marriage into a new life.

Everyone arrived, groaning sympathetically at the grief that had consumed the royal family. A day of public mourning was proclaimed. Reluctantly, the rites of the ceremony were completed in an atmosphere of deep grief. Finally, a distressed yet resigned Psyche led the bridal procession, which included her family and the entire city, to the appointed high place, where limitless sky surrounded the rough earth.

Psyche's parents tried repeatedly to delay the movement of the procession. Psyche knew she had to proceed, however, and found that the pauses, the stumbles, the insistence on the perfect look of the dress, and the stops to share their feelings with friends and strangers only increased her distress. "My poor dear Father and Mother, why torment yourselves by prolonging this grief unnecessarily? Why increase my pain with your pitiful cries? Why torture your throats with uncontrolled shrieking? Why inflame your eyes and swell your lids and cheeks, disfiguring those faces that I hold so dear? Why pound your aging breasts until my own heart breaks from aching? Now, too late, you finally can see the prize you and I have won for all my beauty: the curse of divine jealousy and outrage for the extravagant and misplaced honors paid to me. When people all over the world celebrated me as the new Aphrodite and offered me sacrifices, then was the time for you to grieve and weep as though I already dwelled among the dead.

"In all this turmoil, I now see clearly, as if the fog had lifted to reveal the landscape that always resided there, that a great cause of all this misery, of the drought that has beset the kingdom, of the browning of the crops, of the failure of all things to regenerate in fresh form, is due to the blasphemous use of the goddess's name.

"Come with me now to that craggy place where I am to begin my bridal night with my marvelous husband. Why should I hesitate to have this burden lifted and get on with the happy fate that awaits me? Why should I shrink from this husband who was born with the power to tear apart the world?"

With that, she walked with the resolve of one who anticipates finally discovering her destiny and yet is filled with grief and anxiety. The reluctant family and sorrowful crowds followed her to the rough edge at the top of the mountain, where they moaned their goodbyes and departed for home, dejected, extinguishing the wedding torches with their tears, and stumbling down the hillside as if in a daze. The grief-burdened parents secluded themselves in their palace, retreating into perpetual night by drawing all the curtains.

13

Alone, scared, trembling with sadness and anxiety, Psyche stood waiting on the very edge of the cliff atop her nuptial mountain. The gentle, embracing West Wind, Zephyr, suddenly arose and played around her, swelling her skirt and flapping her sleeves and veil. Gradually, this swirling, unseen, yet felt presence, lifted her from the ground and carried her down the side of the mountain. She was gently laid on a bed of soft low growth studded with welcoming little flowers in the bosom of a hidden valley.

The wonder of being swept away, the fatigue of so many days and months of loneliness, worry, and distress, and the sensual pleasure of resting on such a softly firm natural bed all conspired to relax the brave maid and she promptly fell into a sweet sleep. When she awoke refreshed, it was still daylight. She spotted a bubbling stream flowing among tall trees in a nearby wood and walked calmly along the stream, following it deeper and deeper into the forest. The stream led her to the heart of the wood, where she beheld a dazzling sight, one that kissed her eyes with its radiance and filled her heart with awe at its splendor.

As she passed through the entrance to the clearing, she knew this could only be the residence of a god. Entering the house itself, she noted that the ceiling, exquisitely carved of sandalwood and ivory, was supported by golden columns. Figures of wild beasts, embossed in silver on the walls, seemed to move directly toward her as she gazed at them. A skilled heavenly hand manifested in every remarkable detail. The floor, a pavement of precious stones, formed many kinds of images. The entire house and all it contained demonstrated richness beyond imagination. The walls, constructed of solid gold and adorned by their silver figures, gave off the glow of daylight. Every room, door, and hallway shone with light, as did the furniture. This could have been the earthly abode of Zeus.

As Psyche wandered into and through this divine palace, she filled with wonder at the beauty she beheld and the countless treasures she discovered. Everything that could be desired was contained within its chambers. She looked around, amazed that no one guarded this boundless treasury, that no lock or barrier protected its riches.

As her senses relished the delightful sights, an unseen voice suddenly spoke to her: "My lady, are you overwhelmed by such splendid treasures? They are all yours. Why not go to your bedchamber and rest. Relieve your tired body. Bathe when you like and we, whose voices you hear, will attend to your every need. Having refreshed your body, you can then enjoy a royal banquet we will be pleased to serve you."

Grateful for the good care, Psyche followed the advice and slept. When she bathed, invisible hands undressed her, washed her, massaged the tensions from her shoulders and back, and dressed her again. After the pleasures of the ablutions, a couch shaped like a half moon appeared and she eased herself into a comfortable position. Immediately, nectar wine and tasty dishes magically appeared. When she wanted venison or an apple, it appeared as if on its own. Musicians, like the servants, remained invisible as they serenaded her. Unseen choirs sang in the background as she feasted.

Having satisfied her taste and filled her belly, Psyche felt more at home and more relaxed. She was still tired, however, for it had been dark for some time, so she returned to the bedchamber, undressed, and snuggled between sheets of silk. Around midnight, she was startled by a gentle whispering and began to tremble with fear for her virtue and with a terror of the unknown more than any possible harm. The soft whispering continued as her unknown husband climbed into bed with her. With a sure, yet gentle touch, he took her into his arms and with overflowing heart made love to her. And so they affirmed their relationship as husband and wife.

Before first light, he quietly departed. The unseen voices reassured Psyche of what had transpired—that she had indeed become a wife, losing her virginity but not her virtue. Psyche settled into a delicious sleep as her entire body smiled with satisfaction and delight.

Each day thereafter, Psyche made herself more and more at home and each night she made rapturous love with her unseen husband. This continued for days and weeks and months, and some even say years. As you might expect, the novelty of invisible servants wore off and pleasant routines developed.

Meanwhile, Psyche's parents continued to torment themselves with grief. The news of Psyche's fate and the distress of the king and queen eventually reached the kingdoms of Psyche's sisters. With sorrow in their hearts, they hastened to be with their parents to comfort them.

The very night of the sisters' arrival at their parents' home, Psyche's unseen husband warned her: "Beautiful Psyche, my beloved wife, the Fates are turning cruel and you must beware of deadly danger. Your sisters, alarmed by what they believe is your death and the distress of your parents, will make their way to the ledge from which you were carried to this secret valley. They will search for any trace of you. If you hear their mournful cries, ignore them. Do not answer them or seek them out in any way. For any response to them will drive me into pain, make you desolate, and may destroy our marriage."

Psyche promised to follow her husband's instructions. But after his departure by morning light, the tears of loneliness and familial separation came flooding forth. The poor girl cried the entire day, complaining over and over about being a prisoner in this splendid palace, about not having a single human being to speak to or play with, about being forbidden to give comfort to her family. Neglecting food and forsaking her usual soothing bath, Psyche continued to weep, soaking the pillows of her nuptial bed with the waters of her distress.

Even when her husband arrived and embraced her, she still wept. Upset, he said to her: "Oh dear Psyche, you have cried night and day. What can I expect from you when even my heartfelt embrace does not diminish your anguish?"

Psyche pleaded with him and threatened him with her own unhappiness. She even suggested she would slay herself if she remained isolated from her family. Eventually, her husband reluctantly consented: "Well then, so be it. Do as you like and follow your disastrous inclinations. However, I warn you that, by the time you realize your mistake, the damage will already have been done." In granting her desire, he said he would have the sisters brought to their palace so Psyche could see them and assuage their sorrows and concerns. He also indicated that she could give them as much jewelry as she wished. He went on to warn her insistently that she must never reveal anything about him or their relationship and that she must avoid what he knew would be their selfishly bad counsel. If she listened to them and betrayed the marriage relationship to them, it would mean the end of their present happiness and a rupture in their marriage.

Psyche thanked him for his understanding and kindness and, cheered by the prospect of seeing her family, assured him: "I would rather die than betray us and lose you. While I have no idea who you really are, I love you. I love you as I love life itself. Eros himself could not compare to you. I prefer your kisses to his divine embrace. So please, rest assured and grant me one last wish—that your servant the Zephyr, the West Wind, carry my sisters down to this secret valley in the same manner that I was transported." Then she kissed him most fervently, wrapping him in her legs and arms and making passionate love to him. She called him "dearest husband, sweeter than honey, the soul's very life and love." Overwhelmed by the power of love, he yielded once again. And so the night passed and he vanished before daybreak.

Sure enough, on that very day, the sisters, guided to the ledge, beat their breasts and cried so loudly and mournfully that the rocks echoed their wails. They shrieked, "Psyche, O Psyche what has become of you?" The volume and shrillness of their lament resounded even in the secret valley below and Psyche ran out of her palace with trembling excitement, yelling: "Sisters do not mourn me for I am well and am here. Stop your wailing and wipe your tears; momentarily we shall all embrace."

Then she summoned Zephyr and, with a gentle gust, he carried the sisters from the ledge to where Psyche awaited. They embraced eagerly and tears of joy replaced those of sorrow. "Come see my new home and let's enjoy our time together." As proud mistress of the house, she excitedly showed them all the wonderful rooms. The invisible retinue sang and bathed the sisters. They feasted at the magical table.

Their senses satisfied as they had never been before and awed by the heavenly wealth of their younger sister, the two visitors fell prey to an ugly envy. The more inquisitive of the two set out to find the source of this fabulous prosperity. She pressed Psyche to tell her what kind of lord possessed these marvels; what kind of husband was he and what did he do?

Psyche, loyal to her promise, revealed nothing and made up a story to satisfy her insistent sisters. Without pause and in the most matter-of-fact manner, she declared that his features were handsome with the downy hair of youth and that he spent much of his time hunting in the nearby mountains. When her sisters inquired further, she feared making a slip and contradicting herself, so she changed the subject and offered them handfuls of necklaces, rings, broaches, and other fine jewelry. Then she quickly called upon Zephyr to carry them back to the ledge where they had started the day.

On their way home, the sisters were consumed by a jealousy that eclipsed all other feelings and considerations. The eldest complained: "How unfairly have the Fates treated us, that we, the eldest born to the same parents, should have to endure such different situations. We two, who had to marry foreign rulers, are now in exile from our home and slaves to our husbands. By what right does she, the youngest, deserve such wealth and to have a husband who must be a god? She clearly does not have the sense to make proper use of her overflowing riches. Did you see the mass of jewels and treasures? Why even the floors were gold with inlaid gems. If her husband is as fair and wonderful as she described, this god of hers may even make her a goddess as their love increases. Truly she, of flesh and bones, acts like a goddess now, the way she treats her fortune so casually and can command even the winds. This is an insult. I can feel my hatred growing. And here I am with a husband older than my father, as bald as a pumpkin and weaker than a small boy, who is so afraid that everything is locked up and guarded."

The other sister picked up where the first left off. "My husband is even worse. He is hunched over with deformed and stiff bones and suffers so much from all kinds of pains that he hardly thinks of love. I have become a nurse, having to rub his crooked fingers and aching joints. My hands have lost the softness and texture of youth from all the salves and foul solutions I administer to his deformed body. I have reached my limit. You may have patience with your own servile position and the great fortune of Psyche, but I can endure no longer. What has she ever done to deserve her new station? Remember the arrogance she exhibited in showing us around and how paltry were the gifts she gave us from her vast wealth? And as soon as she was bored, she promptly got rid of us!

"Frankly, as long as the fire of life burns within me, I will not rest until she is brought down from her heights and made to live in the gutter. Join me if you feel as strongly as I do. Let's plan how to humble the wench."

"I support your cause," replied the eldest, "and I suggest that we hide the treasures and the truth about Psyche from everyone, including Father and Mother. We don't want to be the bearers of the news of her good fortune. After all, we are not her servants, but her older sisters."

As they approached the home of their parents, they feigned grief and made excuses to return to their own realms. Consumed by a mounting rage, they wanted time to scheme to ruin their innocent sister, even if that meant her death.

Meanwhile, Psyche's unseen husband admonished her again about the dangers that could come of the visit. One night, he asked her: "Can you not see what great danger you are courting? The terrible storm approaches and, when it hits, it will sweep you away if you are ill prepared. These false-hearted she-wolves are plotting our destruction. They will try to persuade you to look upon my face, which, as I have told you, once done, will tear our relationship apart and you will see me no longer.

"So if these wicked bloodsuckers come again—and I am sure they will—you must refuse their company. If you must see them, give no heed to anything they say about your husband. This is of utmost importance, for we are about to become parents. Your young womb holds a child of your own who will be born divine if you keep our secret. If you divulge what is not meant for them, the little one will be mortal."

Psyche was overjoyed with this news and rejoiced with the thought of bringing a divine baby into the world. Starting that night, she began counting the days as they went by and the months as they passed and exulted at the divine promise that grew inside her.

Yet her two bedeviled sisters were plotting another visit. Her husband once again warned Psyche with increased urgency: "The fateful day is upon you. Those consumed siblings of yours have prepared to battle you and have sharpened their swords for your life's blood. My dearest Psyche, for heaven's sake, for the sake of yourself, me, and our unborn child, keep our sacred secret and protect us all from the turmoil that can ruin this house, this marriage, and the future of our babe. Refuse to see or listen to those conniving sisters, if they can even be called sisters with all the hate they harbor toward you. Ignore their fateful voices when they shout from the rocky heights and do not let them come to our home."

Sobbing, Psyche could barely get out her reply: "You certainly have had proof that I can be trusted. I am even more resolved in our secret than the last time and will demonstrate it once again tomorrow. Please tell Zephyr to obey as before so that I may see my sisters, even if I cannot see you. I delight in the fragrance of the curls that dangle across your brow. I marvel at your smooth cheek, as soft as my own. I draw warmth from the heat radiating from your bosom. I only hope to know your face in the face of our child. So please humor me and my familial longings, and make your Psyche happy. I seek no more to gaze upon your face. In my love, not even the darkness stands in the way of my joy in embracing you, light of my life."

Her words, tones, and sweet caresses removed his will to resist. He wiped her tears with his fine, soft curls and agreed to her wishes. Again, before day broke, he disappeared.

The conspiring sisters, with the outlines of a plan in their scheming heads, made their way to the ledge of departure and confidently leapt out into the air. Zephyr caught them as they fell and safely deposited them on the floor of the secret valley. They rushed into the palace in search of their sister and, with false joy, embraced the innocent mistress of the house. Noting her condition, the eldest said: "My goodness, Psyche, you have become larger. You are no longer a child, but I would guess that you are about to become a mother. What wonderful news to share with Father and Mother! You cannot imagine the kind of joy we have for what is carried in your womb. Surely the blessed babe, if its parents are anything to go by, will be as great as a god like Eros."

So they continued to work their way into Psyche's trust. They spent the day lounging, bathing, listening to music and songs of the unseen chorus, conversing, and finally feasting in the finest fashion.

The harp and flute played sweet melodies as they dined. Yet not even the beauty of the music, which could reach the coldest heart, could deter the two sisters from their destructive purpose.

Interspersed with all the gossip, they kept probing with questions, seeking any information that could be used to advance their cruel goal. In the course of these inquiries, they asked more about Psyche's husband, his family, and his standing in the world. Unwittingly, Psyche, having forgotten the tale she told on their previous visit and not wanting to dwell on this forbidden subject, mentioned that he was a slightly graying and very rich trader from a neighboring province. Not wanting to continue, she then broke off their time together. She loaded her sisters once more with precious presents and sent them away with the wind.

Landing on the ledge and making their descent toward home, they spoke almost in unison: "Can you believe the stupendous lies she told us? First her husband is a fair youth and now he is grizzled and gray. Who could age this way in such short time? Either she is hiding something from us or does not know what her husband looks like or what he does. Whatever the truth, we must bring her down. If she has never seen him, then he must be a god and her unborn child will be born a god as well."

The eldest exclaimed: "If that were to happen, god forbid, I would hang myself in envy. Let's make a quick visit to our parents, without revealing anything, and, now that we have guessed her secret, devise a plan for when we return tomorrow."

Spending only as much time with their parents as was required by duty, the sisters spent an angry, agitated night working out their cruel scheme. At dawn, they hurried to the high ledge and were brought quickly down by the obedient wind. Then, rubbing their eyes to make them red and teary, they frantically approached Psyche: "Oh darling sister, you are so blissfully innocent of the peril you are in. Meanwhile, we are tormented by what we have come to know and are torn with fear for your coming misfortune. We have learned a terrible truth that, being your kin in all things including grievous circumstances, we must share with you without delay. The one who lies secretly in your bed at night is a monstrous winged snake with deadly venom that can make your body go completely limp. Remember what Apollo's oracle said—that you would wed one of the dragon breed? Such is indeed the case. Farmers who hunt the woods of these mountains have encountered him at nightfall coming home after consuming his prey. Many other people also affirm that they have seen him and know of his unsuspecting victims. By all indications from everyone who knows of him, he will not treat you royally and lovingly much longer, but is simply waiting until you are near full term and then he will consume you with the fruit still in your womb.

"There is no time to be lost. You must decide whether to come away safely with us and let us take care of you, or stay with your deceptive, destructive husband until he devours you as well as your child. If you choose to remain in such danger under such secret and monstrous conditions, so be it; at least, we, your loving sisters, have done our duty by warning you and offering a way out for you and your baby."

Alas, poor Psyche was appalled at this terrifying news and her simple and trusting heart was undone. She lost all sense of reason, was swept away by fear, and totally forgot all her husband's warnings and her own promises. Completely overwhelmed by worry, grief, and doubt, she felt herself go pale and her knees buckled. She stammered almost incoherently: "Oh sisters, you are thoughtful to warn me, for, indeed, I have never seen my husband's face or know anything about what he does or where he comes from. I know him only in the soft whispers of night and in the touch of shadow, for he shuns the light. Those who have told you how fearsome he is must be right and I can only accept your words on this, for he repeatedly has told me of dire consequences if I should look upon him. Please advise me.

23

Do not stop with a simple warning. How shall I proceed in this dangerous situation?"

The clever sisters then pressed their advantage now that their goal was within their grasp and Psyche was ripe for any suggestion. The younger spoke up: "Family ties dictate that we should not leave you without help, even if it means our own peril. After long deliberations since yesterday, we have come up with the only safe plan. Take this sword we have brought along and hide it beside your bed. Hide a clear-burning oil lantern where you can reach it. Be very careful to conceal all your preparations. When your husband comes to your bed, wait until he falls asleep and his breathing lets you know that he is deep in slumber. Then, ever so quietly, leave the bed and pick up the lantern from its dark place. Let the light show you where best to use your sword with all the strength you can muster to sever his head from the rest of his body. Once that is accomplished, we will come to bear you, your child, and your treasure to a safe marriage with a decent man."

Seeing that Psyche was convinced and determined to carry out their scheme, they left her alone, filled with fear themselves about remaining where such a horrifying deed was about to be performed. They were helped to the ledge by Zephyr and ran back to the safety and comfort of their respective kingdoms.

Psyche then fell prey to the furies that haunted and stirred up her soul as might be expected of one about to behead her husband and orphan her child. Her feelings were tossed and upended like a small boat among the high swells of a stormy sea. Yet she made her preparations with a firm resolve. She paused at times, worrying about what would happen if she succeeded and what would happen if she failed. A host of distressing passions—terror, daring, impatience, doubt, sadness, and rage—fed her anguish. In all this, she grew to hate the beast she feared even as she loved the husband she had. As night approached, still determined to follow the plan, she made sure the sword and lamp were ready.

After dark had descended, her husband came to their bed and took her in his arms and kissed her. Soon she felt him relax and heard his deep, long breaths of sleep. Although she was normally not very brave or strong, fear made Psyche fierce. She took the lantern and held tightly to the sword of her deliverance. But as soon as the clear light shone on the bed, the great secret was revealed. She beheld the sweetest and gentlest of all wild creatures, Eros himself, the radiant Love God. At the sight of him, the lantern flame sputtered with joy and the edge of the blade retreated in shame.

Psyche was overwhelmed with the splendor of the sight and trembled in dismay at what she contemplated. The horror of it made her faint and pale and she, without thinking, tried to hide the blade in her own heart. As she sought to perform this awful deed, however, the sword slipped from her fingers, horrified by such a crime. Confused and desperate as she was, Psyche gazed again and again at the beauty of her divine husband and a kind of joy and will returned to her being. She beheld his golden hair, washed in scented ambrosia. She looked lovingly at his rosy cheeks and fine, white neck. The radiance of his head and body made all else, including the lamp's flame, seem pale. From his shoulders sprang downy, pure white wings whose feathery fringes quivered delicately even as he rested. The splendor of his body could only have issued from Aphrodite herself.

At the foot of the bed lay this great god's bow, quiver, and arrows. Curiosity seized Psyche and she reached for her husband's sacred weapons. Taking an arrow from the quiver, she touched the point to feel its sharpness. But her trembling hand pressed too hard and she was pricked. The skin was broken and tiny droplets of blood were released. So, unwittingly, Psyche fell in love with Love. Then her passion burned even more fiercely for passion's very lord. Desperate with desire and filled with the ecstasy of love, she climbed upon him and covered him with kisses, trying, even in this consuming passion, not to wake him.

While she blissfully caressed him, the lamp—itself a servant of Love's eye, the invention of some lover to behold its beloved even by night, and itself longing to touch and kiss such marvelous beauty—sputtered a drop of burning oil on the sleeping god's right shoulder. Such impudence, to scald the very god of Love!

Eros leapt from the bed in pain. What a rude awakening. Seeing his secret betrayed, Eros spread his wings and sought to fly off. Psyche seized his right leg and clung to him as he soared toward the heavens, even as he swept through the clouds. But she could not cling forever and the strength of her grip gave out. She fell directly to the earth.

Eros did not immediately flee. Pulled by the bond they had forged in the dark places of their home together, he set down on the top branch of a nearby cypress. Finally, he woefully spoke: "Oh, my beloved foolish Psyche, it was for you that I betrayed the commands of my mother Aphrodite. She wanted me to inflame you with passion for some unworthy man so that you would marry him. But instead, I descended from Heaven to become your lover myself. How well I know now that my actions were thoughtless and brought about this result. I, the famous archer of passions, wounded myself with my own arrows and married a girl who mistakes me for a monster, who tries to sever my head from my heart—this head with eyes that look upon you so lovingly and this heart opened by the joy of being with you. You would take up the very sword that I warned you against. I begged you to beware of those false sisters who turned you against me and guided you so disastrously. They will get their just reward. Your punishment is simply that I will fly away."

With that, Eros soared into the sky. Psyche could only lie on the hard ground and follow the flight of her beloved until he disappeared from sight. She sobbed bitterly and mournfully. She crawled over to a nearby riverbank and flung herself into the swift waters. But the river would have nothing to do with a deed that so defiled life and could anger the god who was known to torch even these waters. Catching Psyche in its current, the river laid her unharmed upon a sweetly flowering bank.

As it turned out, at that moment and in that place, the god of the countryside, Pan, sat with Echo, the mountain nymph. As he caressed her, he also taught her repeated melodious answers to sounds of every kind. A flock of goats grazed with determined looks as their mouths rapidly chewed the lush grass. The goat-footed Pan, aware of Psyche's misfortune, called her over and tried to comfort her: "Most fair maiden, I am but an old rustic shepherd, yet I have learned a thing or two in my time. So, my intuition (some would say my divination) tells me that your faltering walk, pale complexion, repeated sighs, and mournful eyes are the result of excessive love. Hear what I have to say and cease these misguided attempts to end your life so violently. Wipe away your tears and be more cheerful. Plead your case to Eros, the mightiest of the gods. He is a soft-hearted youth and your prayers and earnestness will bring him around."

Psyche made no reply, but bowed respectfully to the deity. She went on her way down a road by the river until she reached a side road that led to the realm where her eldest sister was queen. Upon entering the palace, she had her presence announced to her sister.

After embracing, the queen inquired about what had happened. Psyche, in a matter-of-fact tone mixed with grief, answered: "Of course you remember the advice about the sword and the plan to kill the monstrous dragon who pretended to be my husband. Well, I did as you counseled. But no sooner had I shone the light of my lamp upon our bed than I saw the most divine sight, the son of Aphrodite, Eros himself, lying there in unsuspecting sleep. I was so filled with joy and wonder that I lost my head and could not get enough of him. My passion knew no bounds and all discretion was lost. But then a dreadful accident occurred. A drop of scalding oil from the lamp fell on his shoulder and burned him severely. The pain awakened him immediately and he saw the fire and the sword. He cried out: 'In punishment for your distrust and foul intent, I banish you from my bed. Take with you what is yours. I will marry someone who is trustworthy and fitting, such as your sister'—mentioning your name. With that, he summoned Zephyr to remove me from that marvelous valley and deposited me here."

Scarcely had Psyche completed her little tale, when her sister, insanely envious of her for having slept with a god and wanting to take her place, went to find her husband. She told him that she had just learned of her parents' death and needed to depart at once. And off she went.

With amazing speed, she reached the ledge above the secret valley. Although another wind, not the West Wind, was churning the air, she blindly called: "Here I am, great Eros. Receive me, whom you deem worthy. Great West Wind, Zephyr, bear up thy new mistress and convey me to the palace immediately!" With that, she hurled herself headlong off the high ledge. She never reached that marvelous valley in life or death, for her body was cut to pieces by sharp rocks as she tumbled downward and her remains were scattered over the mountainside and became food for the birds and animals.

Psyche wandered on until she came to the realm where her other sister was queen and told her the same story. This sister, wishing to replace Psyche in Eros' bed, set out at once, hurried to the ledge, leapt off, and died in the same manner as her elder sibling.

Meanwhile, Eros now lay in his mother's house beset with feverish shivers and moaning in pain from the wound he had received. His condition worsened, but he was unable to get help for himself.

A white gull, the kind that skims the surface of the Ocean then dives into the waves, flew off and dove into the depths where Aphrodite had taken refuge in the bosom of the Ocean. Finding the great goddess enjoying a bath, the bird told her that Eros had been wounded severely, lay at her house in anguish, and might never recover. The bird pointed out that, with Aphrodite having retreated from the world and Eros confined to bed, relationships had fallen into disrepair in the world. There was no pleasure or merriment or connections anywhere. Disorder was spreading as the bonds of love were disregarded.

The talkative bird went on and relayed the gossip that Eros had gotten into this mess by having an affair with a young maiden. Aphrodite grew angry with all the news and cried: "So my good lad has a mistress does he! Gull, my good servant, come let me know the name of this creature who has seduced and distracted my simple and not-yet-fully developed boy. Is she one of the Nymphs or Hours? Or maybe one of the Muses or one of my own company of Graces?"

"I cannot say for sure," the gull replied, "but, your great majesty, if I heard tell correctly and my memory serves me well, I believe the story is that your son has fallen desperately in love with a girl called Psyche."

Aphrodite exploded with wrath: "What! He loves Psyche of all women, the pretender of divine beauty, who would challenge my glory? Does the young scoundrel think I am his procuress? For it was I who introduced him to her!"

With these words, Aphrodite rose from the Ocean and went directly to her golden chamber where she found the ailing Eros in bed. As she entered the room, she loudly shrieked: "Is this the behavior that honors and befits your birth and your station? You are indeed a fine credit to our heavenly family. First you trample your mother's, nay your queen's, order to torment her pretender with base passions. Then you have the impudence to embrace her, to sleep with her, and to make her your wife. Now I must endure the fact that this pretender is my daughter-in-law! I suppose you thought I would quietly accept all this. You have assumed you are my heir, but I am not past the time when I can change all that. I can always bear another son, one more capable than you. I can even adopt one of my slaves and invest him with your wings, torch, bow, and arrows, which you have used in such indiscriminate and immature ways. For none of these powers that make up your trappings came from my husband Hephaestus' side of the family.

"The fact is that you have remained untrained and wild and have delighted in creating trouble. You show no regard in targeting your elders with your arrows, including me and your stepfather, Zeus, the greatest of all warriors. You even dare to secure lovers for him to make me jealous. But now, this is all coming home to you with most unpleasant results. You have only begun to experience the taste of bitterness and grief that you must endure because of this marriage of yours."

Eros did not respond to the tirade and so she continued: "I am not sure how to deal with all this. Or to whom I should turn. How shall I restrain and teach you? Must I call upon the help of old Sobriety, whom I have so often offended for your sake? As hard as that might be for either of us, success and satisfaction are sweet no matter what the source. I will ask for her assistance and hers alone. For she will teach you discipline and restraint in your use of your great gifts. The virtue of her ways will clip that unruly golden hair, bind those lovely wings I once bathed in the milk of my own breast, and apply even harsher remedies to your body. Only then will I feel that good has been done and folly has been set right."

Aphrodite then left the house and soon ran into Hera, Queen of the Heavens, and Demeter, Queen of the Earth. They noted how angry she looked and asked why her beautiful smile was hidden behind so fierce a look. "It is good I met you," she replied, "I need you to calm me, for a great fire is burning within. I also need a favor from you. Please see if you can find that creature Psyche, for you have surely heard of the problems she has caused by her affair with my son."

They, of course, knew all about what had happened and attempted to soothe Aphrodite's wrath. Hera asked: "My dear, what great crime has Eros really committed that you would deny his natural impulses and seek to destroy the woman he loves? It is surely no crime to sleep with someone! We all do it."

Demeter added: "You only imagine that he is still a boy because of his youthful demeanor, but you must accept that he is moving on now. We find it strange that you, familiar with the ways of the world, would seek to interfere in his life. You complain about the very powers and impulses that he gets directly from you. Who among the gods would not think you a hypocrite for sowing passions in the world while denying them to your own son?"

The goddesses, themselves fearful of Eros' arrows, came to his defense even as they tried to appease Aphrodite. But she, seeing that they did not understand what was really at stake, indignantly hurried on her way back to the Ocean.

Meanwhile, Psyche wandered day and night, restlessly searching for her husband. She thought that she could appease his anger and remedy the situation with their own special love words, and even by getting on her knees and repenting before him. In the course of her travels, she noticed a temple atop a high mountain. "Perhaps my love dwells in that sacred place," she said to herself. As she climbed the difficult terrain, hope and love filled her heart and gave her strength. Upon surmounting the high ridge, she entered the temple and approached the sacred altar. There she saw offerings of wheat piled in a heap, and ears of barley, sickles, and other harvesting implements all scattered in careless confusion.

She carefully arranged them and placed them in their proper places. She wanted to improve any shrine she came upon out of respect for all the deities and in hopes that they might help her find her beloved. The temple belonged to generous Demeter, who, seeing Psyche working so hard and mindfully, called to her: "I see that it is you, poor Psyche. Aphrodite is furious and searching for you everywhere. She would take you in her mighty grip, eager to teach you a lesson she believes you have long needed. I am impressed that you take the time to look after my affairs without fear for your own situation."

Psyche prostrated herself before the goddess, sweeping the ground around Demeter with her hair and washing her divine feet with her tears. Psyche implored her assistance: "Great Goddess, by your hand that brings the fruit of the Earth, by the joy of the harvest ceremonies, by the silent mysteries of your sacred baskets, by the winged dragons of your chariot, by the furrows of Sicily from which sprang the chariot of Hades to carry Persephone to the Underworld where their wedding was celebrated, by the joyous return of her light to the Earth, and by all the mysteries of Eleusis, help me, please give your aid to your supplicant Psyche. Help me hide from the wrath of Aphrodite until she is calmer. If that be too long to manage, at least give me shelter and refreshment so that I may regain my strength, for I am very tired and have had no rest in my search for Eros and my flight from Aphrodite."

Demeter answered: "Your tearful prayers touch my heart and I would love to give you aid, but I will not cross my kinswoman, who is also one of my best friends. As someone who knows her intimately, I can assure you that she has a good heart, which you will see when you get to know her. You must move on from my temple and count yourself fortunate that I have not kept you here or tried to protect you from her whom you must face."

This unexpected rejection of her plea doubled Psyche's distress and she set off once again into the world, seeking her beloved or at least some refuge. Soon, as she wandered through a sacred forest in a deep valley, she came upon another beautiful temple. Hoping to put things right for herself, she passed through the sacred portals in order to obtain some divine assistance. When she saw the precious gifts, the gold-lettered embroidery hanging from the doorposts, and the splendor of the entire temple, she knew this was all dedicated to Hera in gratitude for the favors people had received from her great mercy.

Psyche fell to her knees and, wiping her tears, placed her hands on the altar, still wet from a recent sacrifice. "Sister and wife of mighty Zeus, wherever you may be, you who are honored as the Queen of Heaven, as the Goddess of Marriage, as the Goddess of Childbirth, and as the most merciful. Please, I beg you, see my great misfortune and rescue me from the fear of imminent danger, for I have endured so much and am very, very tired and quite frightened. I know you always help mothers in trouble."

Hera appeared in all the august majesty of her divine station and replied to Psyche's prayers in this way: "I would gladly honor your prayers and requests. But by the customs of Heaven, I cannot. I would not cross the wishes of my kin Aphrodite, who married my son Hephaestus, as you know. I love her as my own child. I am forbidden to harbor one who is bound to another without their consent and you are surely bound to Aphrodite. It is she you must seek."

Psyche again was filled with despair at these words of rejection. She gave up all hope of staying safe, saying to herself: "Where can I turn for help if even these powerful and kindly goddesses will not assist me? I am so entangled in the snares of my fate that I cannot go on this way. No house, no dark place can hide me from the inevitable gaze of Aphrodite. Come now, take heart and be strong. Your puny hopes are shattered. I will boldly renounce all silly hopes of escape and voluntarily submit myself to the one I reluctantly call my mistress, my sovereign. It may be too late, but I must try to assuage her wrath with my submission and my willingness to do her bidding. And who knows? I may have a better chance of finding my beloved in my mother-in-law's house." And so she prepared herself for the uncertain outcome of her submission, which could mean her destruction. She meditated on the ways to best approach her Mistress.

Aphrodite, meanwhile, had decided to return to Heaven. She ordered her chariot of burnished gold adorned with the subtlest artwork, a wedding gift from her husband, Hephaestus. Four white doves from her attendant flock placed themselves in the jeweled harness and joyously carried their mistress to the highest heavens. Her retinue included sparrows and many small birds that sang sweet harmonies in announcing the arrival of the great goddess.

The clouds parted, the sky opened, and the upper atmosphere joyfully welcomed her as she drove straight to Zeus' royal palace. Before Zeus, she requested the immediate services of Hermes. She was delighted when Zeus assented, and she went to give her charge to Hermes. She instructed him: "Brother, you know I have never undertaken any project without your assistance and you know that I seek my servant who thinks she can hide from me. Simply make a public announcement offering a reward to the person who finds her and insist that my command be obeyed at once. Here is a detailed description of her. Her name is Psyche."

Hermes swiftly did as he was bidden. He spread the proclamation far and wide: "Let all look for a runaway princess, Psyche by name and servant to Aphrodite. If any one can hold her or can reveal her hiding place, let that person meet Hermes. Your reward will be seven sweet kisses from the mouth of Aphrodite herself, with one most exquisitely honeyed from the tip of her delicious tongue."

People all over the world joined the hunt, enticed by the hope of winning such a marvelous reward. Psyche, who also heard the news and watched as people searched for her, decided she must not delay or hesitate. She was already approaching the gates of Aphrodite's abode.

Psyche was greeted at the door by one of her Mistress' servants, Old Habit by name, who shouted at the new visitor: "So you have come at last to realize who your real mistress is, you worthless speck of dust! Don't pretend you didn't know that we have been searching for you. I'm glad you have fallen into my hands instead of another servant's. You are safe with me. Hell has you in its grip now and there will be no delay in your painful lessons, you impertinent sack of water, flesh, and bone." Then Old Habit grabbed Psyche by the hair and dragged her before Aphrodite, even though she made no resistance and was following willingly.

As she beheld Psyche, Aphrodite burst into wild, almost wrathful, laughter. Shaking her head and scratching her right ear, she cried: "So, you finally decided it was time to pay your respects to your mother-in-law? Or have you come to visit your suffering husband who struggles to recover from the wound you gave him? Don't be frightened, for I promise to give you the sort of welcome and hospitality that a good mother-in-law is bound to give her son's wife."

She summoned two of her servants, Anxiety and Grief, and turned Psyche over to their charge so that they might teach many painful lessons. Following the commands of their mistress, they tormented poor Psyche and then returned her to their mistress' divine presence.

Aphrodite once again howled with laughter: "Look how she thinks to move me with pity for her pregnant condition and the hope of appealing to a grandmother's heart. Me, a grandmother, while still in flower at my age! Should the child of this unrefined servant become Aphrodite's grandchild? I would be a fool to call this child a true son. This is not the son of a real marriage, for the two of you were not of equal birth; the wedding in the countryside was unwitnessed and without his father's consent. It cannot now be recognized as legitimate and the issue of this union will be a bastard, even if you are able to bring it to term in the condition you are in."

With that, she flew upon poor Psyche and tore her clothes, pulled at her hair, and shook her until her head nearly came off. Then, pointing to a confused, jumbled heap of wheat, barley, lentils, chick peas, millet, and poppy seeds, she said to Psyche: "You look so wretched that your appearance can no longer suffice to attract a husband, so let's see if you can prove your worth through work. See this pile of seeds all mixed up? Sort out each seed and grain, stacking them all with their own kind. Have the work completed by nightfall." Having made the assignment, Aphrodite departed for a wedding feast.

Psyche sat there motionless, gazing at the stupendously disordered mass. As she sat and sat, a very small ant, a dweller of the open fields, understanding the difficulty of her gigantic task and feeling for Psyche, the wife of Love himself, scurried hither and thither to round up every ant in the region, gathering a great host to assist her in her time of need. Wave upon wave of little creatures worked furiously to separate and restack the entire confused heap, grain by grain. Soon, every grain was piled according to its type, and the ants disappeared from sight.

Aphrodite returned that evening from the feast a bit intoxicated, smelling of sweet perfumes, and adorned in wreaths of roses. When she saw with what marvelous diligence and amazing speed Psyche had completed the task, she said: "This is not the work of your hands nor your doing, but the work of some other force that you have enlisted to do your bidding. We shall yet see what you can really do." She tossed Psyche a loaf of coarse bread and went to bed.

Meanwhile Eros was confined to his room under the care and supervision of Sobriety. Instead of the rich diet that he was used to, he was fed a broth filled with all kinds of herbs to fortify his constitution. The wound of his body was treated with medicines known only to the gods. The wound of his heart had no cure, for grief continually carved and reshaped the contours of his heart, a heart that once had seemed so impenetrable.

Hour after hour he lay with the heartache, allowing the waves of grief to wash over him and the feeling of separation to inform his understanding of what people experience. Every time he got restless and wanted distraction from his woeful state by turning to his old ways, Discipline, that loving, strict teacher and an aspect of Sobriety, reminded him of his present task. Even as he longed to go to Psyche, now abiding in the same house, Discipline kept him in his place.

So the lovers spent a restless night under the same roof, kept apart by the strictures of their common mistress.

When Eos, Dawn, had just begun to ride across the sky, Aphrodite called Psyche and said: "Do you see that grove fringing the bank of the silvery stream, with berry bushes hanging over the water that rushes down yonder mountain? In that place, sheep with golden fleeces wander unattended. I want you to fetch a wisp of the wool of that precious fleece as best you can and bring it to me as soon as you can."

Psyche arose and set off for the mountain. Although she seemed willing, she was not eager to perform the task. Despair once again took hold of her when she caught sight of the fierce golden rams and she thought of flinging herself off a cliff that overhung the river. But a river reed, of the kind used in Pan's musical flutes, was softly blown upon by some divine breeze. It whispered its melodious advice to her: "Pause, Psyche, pause from what you are about to do. I know what sorrows and despair you have endured, but you must not pollute my sacred waters with your willful death. Do not approach those dangerous rams at this time of day. Wait. The heat of the sun infuriates them and they will kill any creature that ventures among them with their sharp horns, their stony heads, and their vicious bite. Wait. In the afternoon, when their strength is spent and a breeze cools their dispositions, and the melodious singing of the stream puts them to sleep, come out of hiding among the trees and gather the wisps of precious wool that can be found on the briars and leaves that they have brushed in their passionate running about."

Psyche gave thanks to the kindly reed and followed its advice. She waited until the appropriate time and gathered just as much golden wool as needed to fill her bosom, and returned to Aphrodite later that afternoon. Aphrodite looked sternly upon her daughter-in-law and gave a knowing grin: "I am quite conscious of the fact that you once again had help from another force."

"Now I will test your courage and prudence," she continued. "Look over there to the summit of that high mountain. Near its peak, the dark stream from the Underworld emerges and cascades down steep slopes into the gorge below, then floods the Stygian marshes and feeds the mournful streams of Cocytus. Take this small urn, fill it with the icy water from the very mouth of that high stream where it gushes forth from the rock, and bring it to me." She gave Psyche an urn of carved crystal and admonished her not to fail in this sacred task.

Psyche rushed off to the top of the mountain. She figured that she would either accomplish the task or have an opportunity to put an end to her despair. As she reached the slopes of that high mountain, she perceived the deathly treacherous nature of the path and the stupendous difficulty of the task. The dreadful waters of the Styx issued forth from rocks higher than she could imagine, above slippery and inaccessible slopes. The river had long ago carved a narrow passage through hollowed boulders, flowing unseen to the gorge below. On both sides of the outlet, she saw fierce dragons pacing back and forth with long necks and unblinking eyes, ever watchful and unaffected by the light of day or the darkness of night. The waters themselves seemed to chant: "Beware. Beware. Take care. Take care. Stay away. Stay away. Death! Death!"

Psyche remained stone still, knowing the deadly peril if she proceeded further in this impossible task. She did not even release the tension of her current predicament through the comfort of tears. Remaining still and in a state that transported her beyond even her fears, Psyche wondered what could possibly arise next.

As it happened, the keen eyes of Providence noticed the plight of the innocent mother and urged the great eagle of Zeus to aid her. Sailing down from the heavens, the royal bird, grateful for the past assistance of Eros, screamed to her: "How simple-hearted and untrained you are that you would contemplate catching or even touching so much as one drop of that most sacred fountain. Have you not heard that even the gods and Zeus himself fear the waters of the river Styx and acknowledge the supremacy of that holy river of life and death? Come, give me the urn!"

The royal bird then snatched the small jar and soared to where, in his panoramic vision, he could see the flowing source of life. He swiftly maneuvered his way between the rows of snapping jaws and forked dragon tongues. The river sought to prevent him from dipping in its waters and warned him of the danger. He explained that he was in service on a mission for the great Aphrodite. The river allowed him to approach and he filled the urn and returned to Psyche. She, in turn, carefully and joyfully made her way back to the palace and gave the precious water to Aphrodite.

Even this remarkable deed did not satisfy the determined goddess. Aphrodite resolved to require a still greater task. Smiling sweetly, she said to Psyche: "You must be a great and powerful sorceress to have carried out my orders so precisely and so easily. But I still have one more task for you to accomplish, dear girl. Take this box and go down to the Underworld, down to the palace of Hades. Give it to Persephone, saying, 'Aphrodite sends her greetings and requests you to send a small portion of your beauty in this box, just enough for a brief day. Her own store has been depleted by having to sit up nights caring for her wounded son.' Make sure you come back quickly, because I must use it before I appear at the great theater on Olympus."

To Psyche, this seemed the end of it all, for her orders were clearly meant to take her directly to the home of death. She immediately made her way to a high tower, figuring that the swiftest and most direct way to the Underworld was to throw herself from its height.

Before she could proceed, however, the tower spoke to her: "Poor child, do you really want to end your life from here? That would be a rash act of despair when you are so close to completing your trials. If you kill yourself and force the breath to leave your body, you will surely go to Tartarus, the Underworld, but will have no way of returning. Listen carefully and I will instruct you. On the outskirts of the city of Lacedaemon is Taenarus, a place off the beaten path and hidden from view. There you will find a cave and, in it, a deserted path leading to the Underworld. Climb through that threshold between the worlds and follow the path directly to the palace of Hades. It is vital that you bring two pieces of barley and mead cake with you, and keep two coins in your mouth.

"When you have gone a good distance along the road, you will meet a lame ass loaded with wood. Its lame driver will ask you to assist him in reloading a few branches that have fallen from the load. Do not stop or speak with him. Continue until you reach the river of the dead. There, Charon will request a fee to carry you in his small boat. Yes, avarice thrives even in that world of the dead and a poor man who cannot pay will linger on this side of the Styx unable to make the final crossing. In any case, give the filthy ferryman one coin, but he must take it from your mouth not your hand.

"While you are crossing the sluggish river, a dead man will beg you to take his hand and pull him into the boat. You must not give in to pity, for that would cause you to violate the laws of that world. When you reach the far shore, three women weaving the web of fate will invite you to help them with their great cloth. You must not touch that forbidden cloth. These are all snares to trap you in that world by getting you to drop one of the barley cakes that are critical to your survival on this journey. For these cakes are for Cerberus, the fierce, three-headed hound that howls to frighten the dead, even though they are beyond threats. This great beast keeps constant watch at the threshold of Persephone's palace. Throw him one of the small cakes and, as the heads fight for the one piece, slip past him and into the very presence of Persephone. You will be warmly welcomed and invited to sit awhile in a comfortable chair and share a great feast. Instead, sit on the hard ground, ask for a piece of bread, and eat nothing else. Then deliver your message and she will give you what you came for.

"In returning, again toss a small cake to the hound, pay Charon the other coin, and quickly, without pause for any reason, ascend the path by which you came until you can once again see the sky. Oh, and by the way, under no circumstances seek to find out the nature of the divine treasure in the box you are transporting."

Psyche took the advice of the divinely inspired tower. She rushed to Taenarus carrying the two small cakes and the coins. She entered the dark cave and ran down the road to the Underworld. As instructed, she passed in silence the lame man and his lame mule, paid Charon the first coin, ignored the entreaties of the corpse, refused the invitation of the weavers, distracted the hound with the first cake, and presented herself to Persephone. Inside the great palace, she thanked Persephone for the offer of a soft chair and wonderful meal and chose to sit on the ground and eat only simple bread. She delivered the message from Aphrodite, and Persephone took the small casket and went to fill it in a secret chamber, out of Psyche's sight. Psyche thanked Persephone and departed with the box under her arm. She silenced the barking hound with the second cake, paid the second coin to the old mariner, and ascended from the world of the dead with a far lighter and more joyful step than when she had descended. Upon reaching daylight, she gave lavish prayers of praise for its brilliance and beauty.

As she hurried on her way, she became distracted by compulsive curiosity. "I wonder what this divine beauty is," her mind said to itself. "I'll bet that, if I take a very small amount of it for my own preparation for my beloved, it won't matter and will never be noticed." So she opened the small casket, but it did not appear to contain beauty or anything else. In fact, an invisible Stygian sleep was released that overwhelmed her, wrapping her in a thick fog of drowsiness. She fell right there in the path back to Aphrodite's palace, lying motionless like a corpse.

Eros, healed of his wound, disciplined by the training of Sobriety, and more compassionate from the experience of his own grief, could bear his separation from his beloved Psyche no longer. When he saw her lying on the path to the palace, he flew through the open window of his bedroom retreat. His refreshed wings spread with joy at the restored freedom of movement and carried him faster than ever. He landed at Psyche's side, gathered the sleep that covered her, and placed it in the small box. Then he lovingly, gently, and harmlessly pricked her with one of his arrows.

"My dearest love, curiosity almost destroyed you a second time. Yet, last time you awakened me and now it is my turn to awaken you. Quickly now, complete the task that my mother set for you and I will attend to everything else that is needed." With that, Eros rose upon his wings and Psyche ran to deliver the gift from Persephone to Aphrodite.

Eros, filled with great love and renewed determination, flew to the very highest Heaven and placed himself at the feet of Zeus, where he pleaded for the support of the great god in his marriage to Psyche. Zeus smiled with amusement, pinched Eros' cheek, and kissed his hand. "My son and master, you never before have paid me the respect that is due to my station. In fact, you have mischievously wounded my heart, which has responsibility for the order and harmony of the elements and the constellations of the sky. You have embarrassed me by consuming me with earthly lusts. You hurt my good name by tempting me with mortal adulteries that undermine public order. I get so affected by your arrows that, in my lust,

I transfigure my royal appearance into that of serpents, fire, wild beasts, swans, and cattle. And yet, I cannot forget how often I played with you on my knee and held you in my protective arms. I am softhearted, so I'll help you and give you my full support. But I warn you that you must protect yourself against rivals who may envy you and be taken by your beautiful wife. Also, remember the one who now helps you and be on the lookout for any women of surpassing beauty so you can introduce us."

Giving Eros a fatherly pat, he called upon Hermes. "Summon all the gods to an assembly. Let it be known that attendance is mandatory." The grand theater of the Heaven filled immediately. Great Zeus, sitting above all on his high throne, proclaimed:

> Honorable gods and goddesses whose names are recorded in the register of the Muses, you all know the young fellow here whom I have raised from boyhood and whose passionate nature needed curbing in some way. You need no reminding of the reputation he has for leading so many into vices. Now it is time for him to leave those wild ways and embrace the virtues of a divine marriage. He has found and seduced a maid called Psyche, and now he must keep her forever. Let him be satisfied with this love for all eternity.

Turning to Aphrodite, the great god added: "And you, my daughter, who have worked so hard to teach this mortal a divine lesson, have no fear that this marriage will diminish your lineage. For I will see to it that this is clearly a marriage of equals as it should be." He then turned to Hermes and said: "Fetch Psyche and bring her to heavenly Olympus." When she arrived, he welcomed her warmly and offered a goblet of divine nectar. "Drink, Psyche, and become immortal. Eros shall never again leave your arms and your marriage shall endure forever."

Hephaestus cooked the wedding meal. The Hours decorated the wedding hall with roses and flowers. Presently, a great wedding

43

feast was laid out. Eros and Psyche reclined at the place of honor with her head resting on his heart. Zeus and Hera lay side by side and all the gods took their proper places. Zeus was served the nectar of the gods by Ganymede, his personal cupbearer; Dionysus served everyone else. The Graces sprinkled balsam water, and the Muses chanted the marriage hymn accompanied by the flute and pipe music of Satyr and Pan. Aphrodite danced in celebration of the happy occasion. In this marvelous fashion, Eros and Psyche were properly married and shortly a child was born to them whose name was Rapture.

How the heavens sang and all on Earth vibrated with the resonance of the beautiful child, Rapture, also known as Bliss, Ecstasy, Divine Pleasure, and Delight. Rapture was the fulfillment of the deepest longings for a sense of harmony, transcendence, love, and grace. As the child grew, the pleasure of her Wisdom presence inspired poets, spiritual seekers, philosophers, and followers of the hidden arts. For those who successfully navigate the challenging seas charted in this story, Rapture takes up residence in their hearts and transforms their experiences, sharpens their perceptions, heightens their senses, and intensifies their sense of being. The chosen, who qualify themselves through hard work and perseverance, are graced with a loving, compassionate heart, a wonderfully outrageous sense of play, and a serenely confident engagement in the fullness of life.

Rapture, as Ecstasy, *ekstasis*, transforms everything that comes within the field of her gaze, her hearing, or her touch. All earthly experience is simultaneously viewed as sacred. She carries the fire of her father and the life force and learning of her mother. She arises in the hearts of all those who follow the path of her divine parents.

Chapter Three

THE VALUE OF MYTH

*The resurrection of the soul is accomplished by bringing
together only the purest essence of our bodies or matter into
the light of meditation and reflection on life experiences.
It becomes a permanent and always available state of consciousness that embodies the highest aspirations and
evolution of mind and is sensed as a new strength
of personality to survive any onslaught.*

DENNIS WILLIAM HAUCK

While the myth of Eros and Psyche reveals universal life
principles, I find its Greek flavor makes it more accessible to Westerners because it resonates in familiar
ways with certain sensibilities and fits the contours of Western culture. Over the forty years that I have worked with this myth, first
attempting a screenplay based on it and later using it to teach spiritual retreats, a clear mapping of psycho-spiritual development
emerged. In my teachings and writings on this subject, I have
drawn heavily on my own experience as a spiritual practitioner and
indirectly on the teachings of my teachers, who are based primarily
in the Eastern traditions of Buddhism, Tibetan Bön, and Taoism. In
addition, I have been informed by years of interest in Kabbalah and
Western alchemy.

Far from it being a curious story of another time, I suggest that the teachings in this myth are relevant to all who desire self-understanding and are sincerely dedicated to the task of spiritual transformation. To realize the depth and wisdom of the myth requires a careful reading and hard personal work. Apuleius, the second-century author of the story on which this and most other retellings are based, was part of a highly complex religious and mystical tradition that thrived in North Africa at the time. This story and its interpretations are only introductions to that tradition.

The Transformations *of Apuleius*

Many have speculated that the tale of Eros and Psyche is an ancient Greek myth or folktale that was passed down orally through generations and finally written down as part of a novel. The work, *The Golden Ass*, was written by Lucius Apuleius, a second-century author and practiced rhetorician who was an initiate in the Egyptian cult of Isis and Osiris. He was born in Madaura, North Africa, in 125 C.E. to a wealthy family of Greek origins. He was educated at the university in Carthage, a center for philosophy, the arts, and religious cults. During this period, the dominant center of learning was along the coast in Egypt at Alexandria. The practices of the cult of Isis were known throughout this region and appear to have heavily influenced Apuleius. He was also shaped by his studies in Athens, particularly in Platonic philosophy. He later studied in Rome, where he learned Latin, the language of his writings.

North Africa, where Apuleius grew up and lived much of his life, was a place where Egyptian, Greek, Hebrew, and Roman cultures interacted and influenced each other.[1] The mystery schools thrived in places like Alexandria, home of the greatest library of the ancient world, as well as cities like Carthage. There was a great deal of cross-fertilization between philosophies and religions that included the Hellenized Egyptian practices related to Isis and

Osiris, the Greek practices of Pythagoras, the philosophies of Plato and Aristotle, the Hebrew practices that later became codified as Kabbalah, the Roman revisions of Greek worship, and the growing movement of Christianity.

Apuleius called his larger novel, of which the tale of Eros (Cupid, in Latin) and Psyche was a part, *The Transformations of Lucius Apuleius of Madaura*, later shortened to *The Golden Ass*. For Apuleius, the Eros and Psyche story is a coded version of the secret initiation practices referred to later in the novel when the main character, Lucius, becomes a priest in the cult of Isis. The spiritual mysteries were always coded in stories so that the words and practices that had the power of the "keys" to heaven were concealed from non-initiates. The story of Eros and Psyche gives a basic road map of the steps of alchemical initiation into the mystical circle of Isis.

While my interest centers more around alchemy and initiation, and thus in the story of Eros and Psyche, than the overall novel, the story of Lucius supports a spiritual interpretation of the Eros and Psyche myth, just as the tale itself supports a spiritual interpretation of *Transformations*. Apuleius, while writing in the form of entertainment for a Roman audience, embeds in the characters and sequence of the tale the ancient mythological meanings and mystical sacred teachings.

The novel traces the adventures of Lucius, a man with no experience in the mysteries, whose curiosity about the magical arts accidentally gets him turned into a donkey. Apuleius, in his alternate title, lets us know that he is no ordinary beast of burden, however, but one who journeys toward a supreme reward of a kind of gold.

In the novel, Lucius, as a donkey, becomes the property of robbers, millers, priests, and entrepreneurs, until the grace of Isis transforms him back into human form. He then devotes himself to learning all the mysteries of the cult of Isis, becomes an initiate, and serves the goddess and her consort, Osiris.

The novel teaches that exposure to the magical arts is not the same as the spiritual alchemical practices. It is the journey of learning that Lucius takes from his stumbling beginnings, through his deadly dangerous travails, to his awakening, final initiation, and realization of the true divinity. It also teaches many other lessons. Lucius' curiosity and willingness to take risks are the positive aspects of his venture into the magical at the beginning of *Transformations*, even though he is accidentally transformed into a donkey. This mistake and others along the way lead to dangers, misfortunes, and trials, but eventually to the divine, showing that initiates must be prepared by challenge, by failure as well as success, and must have acquired stamina, strength, perspective, gratitude, and a mature love and respect for the sacred. Lucius has all of these by the end of his journey. Initiation requires hard work, risk, action vs. reaction, virtue as training, and willingness to be subjected to abuse by those who do not understand.

Lucius finally finds a safe "harbor of peace" as he stands "before the altar of loving-kindness." During a dark retreat of the initiation into the priesthood of Isis, he sees radiant sacred light. "At midnight, I saw the Sun shining as if it were noon." He realizes that the true knowledge or wisdom of divinity resides "deep in my heart." After proper preparation, the great god Osiris can be seen directly, not in disguise. This direct knowing requires great inner capacity that is only developed through concentrated meditation and service to the sacred. When Isis finally helps Lucius with his transformation from a donkey and sponsors his subsequent initiation as a priest, she reveals herself, saying:

> I am Nature, the universal Mother, mistress of all the elements, primordial child of time, sovereign of all things spiritual, queen of the dead, queen also of the immortals, the single manifestation of all gods and goddesses that are. My nod governs the shining heights of Heaven, the wholesome

sea-breezes, the lamentable silences of the world below. Though I am worshipped in many aspects, known by countless names, and propitiated with all manner of different rites, yet the whole round earth venerates me.

Among the names she mentions is Aphrodite. Then she says: "The Egyptians who excel in ancient learning and worship me with ceremonies proper to my godhead, call me by my true name, Queen Isis."[2]

Within the novel, the old woman who tells the story is a servant cook for robbers who have kidnapped a young bride named Charite on her wedding day. Charite is held for ransom and is frightened by a dream in which her husband is killed by the thieves as he attempts to rescue her. The old woman tells her not to let the dream frighten her, because dreams are often contrary to reality. She then offers the story of Cupid and Psyche as an example of how things are not always what they seem and how the story turns out well in the end.

It is testimony to the universality of the story, whatever its origins, that so many different commentators from so many different traditions have found meaning and power in its telling. Its images are so evocative that it moves some to identify and learn from Psyche, and others to identify with the example of Eros. Still others recognize the critical role of Aphrodite.

I consider the myth of Eros and Psyche to be a metaphor for the growth and transformation of a dedicated seeker of sacred wisdom and spiritual embodiment. From a spiritual point of view, this myth concerns the sacred development of a human being more than the course of gender development. The process of spiritual maturity transcends gender, and I am wary of imposing contemporary gender concepts on a second-century story when such ideas had no place in the culture and intellectual milieu of that time. Moreover, Apuleius wrote his novel, of which this story is a piece, about the adventures of a man who eventually is initiated into the cult of Isis and Osiris. Most psychological analyses of this story have tended to impose their own theories of gender and human development on it,[3] often ignoring the context of the times, the Hellenistic philosophy that informed Apuleius, and the sacred uses of the myth by those who understood its symbolism and references.[4]

While I believe we can learn something from a literary analysis of the story and from its historical place in the evolution of Western culture,[5] the core teaching of the myth vibrates with the energy of the sacred and sounds a clarion call to experience initiation into the mysteries and consciously work toward spiritual realization. Apuleius says as much by giving the main character of the novel his own first name, Lucius, and referring in his introduction to the work as "my Transformations."

In the time of the ancient Greeks, Romans, and Hebrews, what we now call mysticism was integrated into practical life, not relegated to the edges of culture and society. The sacred infused everything in daily life, and science was married to religion—not in some naïve way, but as an expression of profound wisdom. The foundations of philosophy, theology, alchemy, and spiritual practice were laid in these times no less than the foundations of what we now call mathematics, chemistry, physics, astronomy, biology, rhetoric, and logic.

As we enter into the heart of the story, it assails the defenses of our mind and our reactive habits and seeks to wrest a victory for life and growth from the inertia of our daily habits and confusion. It initiates us into a world far more vibrant, rich, and nourishing than the one we knew in childhood—the one we now naïvely, yet regressively, settle for. In this sense, the story reveals what happens as we attempt to spread our emotional wings in the developmentally confining domain of our childhood home and community, and what it takes to make something significant of ourselves in ways that feed the future. As guests of the story, we discover the larger sacred garden, in which we each emerge as a unique beautiful flower in a bed of exquisite blossoms, each one unique and essential.

According to the myth, your unique contribution to the whole, the result of the alchemical marriage at the end, comes, not so much from what you are given—the beauty, royal birth, and fame that both Eros and Psyche have—but from the wounds you receive, the difficulties you confront, your surrender and service to what seems terrifying but is simply unknown and mysterious to you, and the steadiness of your intention to pursue what you love.

The story celebrates the possibilities and strength of the loving spirit, affected and afflicted by fear, rage, addiction, and longing, but never entirely overcome by these forces. It challenges us toward a re-vision (literally, a new sight) and then a revision of our prior sense of reality. While the forces of numbness and reaction cannot extinguish the sparks of the sacred, they force our spiritual nature to make its sacred way through the oppressive tunnels of incomplete grief and unlived experience. As we take this journey, we have no way of knowing whether the approaching events of life will lead to freedom or death, but we can determine that we will use them as a vehicle to further our growth.

From a mythological and spiritual point of view, all forms—from plants to fish to animals, from mountains and valleys to the sun, moon, stars, and sky, from wind and rain to shining days and darkest nights, from the known and seen to the unknown and invisible, from the most mundane to the supremely sacred—are all collectively dancing, flowing, storming, emerging, and receding in the body of human experience and growth.

In the context of human experience, the story of Eros and Psyche reveals the role of love in the making of meaning and the maturing of relationships. It describes the path to a deeper realization of the potential residing within us and waiting in the nut of our experience to be cracked open and released so it can be digested in the spiritual intestines of a sacred body. Its theme, as in most of the mystic traditions, integrates passion and love with the spiritual, calling on us to live all of life intimately and erotically. This marriage of aliveness and love in the context of the sacred constitutes the erotic, where we experience everything, not only sex, with wholehearted intimacy and engagement. This greater, sacred meaning of the erotic animates the core of this story, suggesting that the divorce of our sensory and passionate nature from our spiritual nature can lead to despair and distortions in the way we live.

The myth describes both a vital dynamic within an individual human and the cycles in a relationship. At another level, it indicates the relational dimension of all existence, and places all of these dynamics and relationships in the context of the sacred. In one sense, mythologically, Eros is not the god of love, desire, and bonding; he is Love that can arise out of desire and bonding. Psyche does not merely symbolize an animating quality; she is the Life Force manifest in people, animals, trees, and plants that must grow through uniting with the creative and connective energies of Eros and Aphrodite.

From a spiritual point of view, we have the responsibility to manifest these divinities by performing our conscious roles in the world. Each of us is an agent of the gods. Each lives with the powerful seeds of love, connection, growth, and regeneration within. Our lifelong task is to plant those seeds in the garden of our experience, feed them, trim them as they grow, and expose them to the warmth and light of conscious attention.

In a sense, Eros and Psyche express the challenge of Love to grow, from the impulse of desire, to the full possibilities of a committed relationship with life as part of a community. At the same time, the story describes the struggles of Psyche, as the Life Force, to grow beyond the ordinary into a creator of meaning and joy through working with the sacred aspects of Love under the guidance of the harsh taskmaster Aphrodite.

52

The myth also reveals our true home, as an embodiment of the Life Force (Psyche), married to Love (Eros), in the company of gods, a member of the community of sacred forces and beings. We not only possess the qualities of life, love, meaning, and connection; we are possessed by them. When we surrender to the demands of these divine elements, we find our authentic home—where we belong, can create value, can host the visitation of experience, can be hosted by the beauty of the divine, and will contribute our unique gift to the larger story of life.

The tale also describes the qualities and stages we go through as an emergent member of a sacred community. The larger context is not you, the individual, but the community to which you contribute through your participation and your legacy. The story describes the maturation of the soul into a contributing member of both the sacred and material worlds.

In working with the story, and in being worked by its mythic qualities, I have come to appreciate how, like an artichoke whose feathery yet barbed leaves conceal a delicious heart that grows from a sturdy stalk, it offers itself for a peeling away of its many meanings and invites you to eat and grow from its precious core. As Martín Prechtel so often points out, the characters in the story are not the heroes, even with their great courage and deeds; the story itself is the hero.

Chapter Four

LEVELS OF MEANING

*It is the imagination that we discard in our youth as having
no value; it is the imagination that is familiar to all, both
rich and poor; it is the imagination which is hidden and yet
known to everyone; it is the imagination that is
"a stone and no stone."*

DENNIS WILLIAM HAUCK

Working with the myth of Eros and Psyche is like play-
ing with a Russian matrushka doll: You open one and
there is another inside, you open that one and there is
yet another, and so on. Over the many years of my work with this
myth, I continue finding new worlds of meaning nested within earlier interpretations. I have come to realize the many layers of
meaning and response contained in the gift of this story. One of
the ways I have explored the myth over the years is by retelling it
and letting it "work" me, furthering my growth as a meditation
practitioner.

The myth of Eros and Psyche is a legacy passed down through
time. In both its oral and written forms, it has remained a treasure
hidden in the cave of a larger story that can only be discovered by

those who know the way. Indeed, the story itself holds the keys to unlocking its meanings at various levels. A literary analysis may open many of the surface meanings and the relationship of those meanings to the larger context of Apuleius' novel and the body of his work.[1] A mythological analysis and an interpretation from a sacred point of view reveal other dimensions of meaning accessible to those trained to recognize them or familiar with the traditions of initiation, spiritually transformative processes, and mystical ways of thinking.

The story invites the listener into a world of paradox, complexity, love, pain, betrayal, loss, and grief. It tells of challenges met, tests failed, and the towering figures of gods and goddesses. Its characters are not meant simply to be observed as curiosities, but rather to be engaged as guides and teachers with whom we establish an intimate relationship and converse as partners in the endeavor of life. As in true conversation, if we listen only to external voices, we remain ignorant of the truths and depths of our own experience; if we listen only to ourselves, we remain ignorant of the truths and possibilities offered by the vast and profoundly rich sources beyond our experience, consigning ourselves to the limitations of our current understanding.

The myth of Eros and Psyche is a tale in which you are required to find the deeper meanings and to extract and practice the teachings within those depths. It is not one of these sacred stories that oblige you to respond with devotion and submit to a set of beliefs. It does, however, reveal a path of practice you can follow and confirm through your own experience.

Although all stories require active engagement, mythology, in spite of its simple form, is especially demanding. In myth, you are constantly asked to live in and beyond the story. Imagination catalyzes the process as you move beyond the obvious into the invisible dimensions of both the outer world of life around you and the inner world of your own experience.

Mythology is a reciprocal art. You invest the story with vitality that draws energy from your mind and heart. The tensions in the story challenge you with paradox as you strive to make sense of apparent contradictions and the swings between hope and despair. You, the listener, are the primary initiate, even more than the characters in the story—just as Lucius, in the context of Apuleius' novel, is the initiate, listening to the story of the old woman. You, as listener, are initiated into the dimensions beyond time and space—the sacred—not only through your identification with Psyche or Eros, but through the story itself, which reveals the eternal aspects of reality. (These dimensions are dynamic but not necessarily linear. Linearity is what makes you mortal.)

As a spiritual and sacred interpreter of myth, you must always be cautious about simplistic conclusions and delve deep beneath the surface appearances of the story. The characters are not always what they seem at first glance. As a conscious listener, you conceive of the story as a universe in which the protagonists, Psyche and Eros, evolve from an immature state to a mature one in which they integrate into the entire cosmic order. You, in turn, perceive that each and every character in the story has a real and important function to play in this evolution.

The storyteller is trying to tell you something with images and themes that are rooted in an invisible reality. This reality is another dimension of life that exists simultaneous with and parallel to your everyday sensory experience. It reflects your past evolution, your future possibilities, and your current state of choices. In other words, the language of the myth draws on the visible world (the one that everyone shares), amplifies those images and insights that have been passed down through generations, and through them says something relevant and profoundly moving about the invisible qualities of life, meaning, and ways of being.

Myths contain characters, gods, and animals that you recognize as part of life, but in a different state of being, expressing a multitude of layers of meaning. They include figures expressing feelings that you recognize, but in a context that is both ordinary and extraordinary. They bring certain qualities to life and destroy others in the course of the story.

Myths use metaphors and images that speak of a reality that is sane and enlightening, not one that is reactive and numbing. They draw us toward an ever-more-comprehensive aliveness, rather than letting us continue our destruction of the sacred through unconscious reactions and addictions to comfort.[2] As this particular myth unfolds, it shifts progressively from the familiar to the mysterious, from a reactive emotional engagement in the story to a glimpse of the possibility of something new, fresh, and counter-intuitive.

Working with the Mythic Puzzle

Myths contain the pieces of a giant puzzle called life—a puzzle that confronts us with an obligation to integrate all its pieces, even when it seems some of the critical pieces may be missing and, we fear, lost forever. Myth-makers are much too honest to pretend that we can find our rebirth in a simple ceremony, dream, or moment of revelation. They don't let us avoid the hard work that must be done to wean our body of habits we have accumulated over a lifetime. In the tale of Eros and Psyche, as in the larger story of *Transformations*, we know the story is leading somewhere, but the promise seems uncertain until we have actually made the journey and gone beyond the trials. This is not a story of easy flight into a happy and loving tomorrow. While the truths are simple and have always been available, our understanding and realization of them is far from certain, and our embodiment takes form only as we make the long and difficult journey.

The bewildering maze of imagery and codes in Western alchemical writings intentionally convey the view that the great work of personal transformation involves both intellectual challenges and concerted effort to extract, not only the deeper meanings of the writings, but the treasures hidden beneath the surface of experience, emotions, and life itself. The story of Eros and Psyche moves us from sight to insight as we progress from a fresh clarity, to a new understanding, to even finer clarity, to wisdom. If we make our journey match the progression of the story, we gradually assimilate more of the qualities and energies of the heavens. Eventually, we want to bring these sacred qualities and energies to the world. This is the essence of alchemical lore.

The myth also promises that we will fail in some way, and that our failures are occasions for support and connection, as when Psyche is overcome as she opens the small casket from Persephone, and is assisted by Eros to emerge from a deadly sleep. Together, with other practitioners, we will succeed. What we realize is that the process of sacred formation and meaning is a collective one that needs to be embodied by the individual and the community. The story describes how an unformed Psyche (Life Force, personal soul) can move from an unconscious state to a sacred position through marriage with Eros (Love, relationship, and primal creation) under the guidance of Aphrodite (the heart of all life and the wisdom of the sacred) and become a member of the assembly of sacred influences in the world as a Sacred Soul.

As we seriously enter the path of spiritual maturity, we must turn ourselves over to the guidance and influence of more accomplished masters. We then take on a paradoxical heart posture in which we surrender our own efforts, even as we work to allow the powers of the sacred to work us. We work in order to be worked.

Unraveling the Meaning

In a sense, this book follows the great tradition of *hermeneutics*, the art of interpreting the meaning of literary works and sacred stories, particularly what lies hidden beneath the surface.

In texts that map out the tasks of transforming consciousness, there are often at least two levels of meaning—the mundane and the sacred. In many cases, the sacred meaning is either the opposite of the mundane, or at least carries an association entirely different from it. This is also referred to as the higher and lower world of perception. For example,

SACRED MEANING	MUNDANE MEANING
Suffering as a sacred truth	Suffering as rooted in ignorance
Darkness as primal source and potential	Darkness as ignorance
Surface beauty as delusion	Surface beauty as attractive
The body as vehicle for sacred work	The body as vehicle for pleasure and pain
Concepts as distractions	Concepts as understanding
Styx as river of life	Styx as river of death
Underworld as fire of purification	Underworld as doomed place of pain
Hades as stage of developing consciousness	Hades as sorrow

In this myth, two stories, one on Earth and the other in Heaven, are identified at the beginning. The stories of the ordinary and the sacred worlds come together in the hidden valley with the initial union of Eros and Psyche, then separate, then merge again when Psyche enters the palace of Aphrodite, then separate momentarily when Psyche is stuck on Earth on her return from the Underworld, and finally unite with the divine wedding.

In addition to the alchemical transformations that the story as a whole represents, it also traces the development of Psyche as a "personal soul" into a "Sacred Soul." The former relates to the capacity in us to learn and grow. The latter encompasses our potential for profound wisdom and the embodiment of sacred qualities. The three meanings of "psyche" in Greek—Life Force or animating quality, soul, and butterfly—suggest that the character of Psyche is meant to connote all of these.

Another lesson in the story refers to the fact that we all face loss, abandonment, disappointment, pain, and harsh treatment. Beyond whatever issues of justice may arise, each of us must still live our life and make ourselves a vehicle for the divine. Every wound does not dictate that you heal it; the wound may be calling you to attend to the sacred evolution of your time on earth. Wounds inevitably happen in the course of living. In fact, it is partly through wounds that the story unfolds and the sacred is made manifest.

The story asks you to become wholehearted—to risk everything for what you cherish. This is what Psyche does over and over in her work to reclaim her love and to become a member of the sacred community. This wholehearted work prepares her for the responsibilities of such membership. It is one thing to find the treasure, another to recognize it, and still another to know how to use it responsibly and skillfully.

Responsibility and service both guide you on your path and complete your initiation into the sacred. The gods are all servants. Psyche moves from being served as a princess to serving the gods as part of her training toward the realization and embodiment of wisdom. She must serve Demeter and Hera and, most important, Aphrodite before she can serve all life.

My mother used to say: "When you have lemons, make lemonade." This is, in fact, an alchemical principle. From a conscious-work point of view, responsibility centers around creating benefit from what is, making the necessary effort, and developing and applying skill. In line with the alchemical principle of turning lead into gold, you consciously make the effort to take the conditions of life, your own and others, and improve them by being an encouraging and loving presence, by healing fractures in relationships, by contributing to the well-being of others and the world, and by creating beauty. In this alchemy of responsibility, you transcend yourself on behalf of others, a community, the world, and the sacred. It is a kind of self-surrender.

PART TWO

The Alchemy of Living

Chapter Five

MYTHOLOGICAL ARCHETYPES

We do not believe in the reality of Olympus, so the ancient Greek gods live on in us as symptoms. We no longer have thunderbolts of Zeus, we have headaches. We no longer have the arrows of Eros, we have angina pains. We no longer have the ecstasy of Dionysus, we have addictive behavior. Even though we no longer recognize the gods we experience their powerful forces.

CARL JUNG

Myths provide a metaphoric guide to profound understanding about the personal, collective, and sacred journeys of life. All stories that can be classified as myth are metaphors for the deeper truths and understandings about self, relationships, and the world. These truths and understandings constitute a profound wisdom that we learn from, grow into, and eventually, with conscious work and connections to teachers and masters past and present, come to embody.

Myths develop gradually as a product of collective imagination and experience. In the course of time, certain motifs emerge, and are elaborated and refined as people tell and retell the stories. The more universal themes and elements that are applicable through time are kept alive by the regular telling, while the particulars inserted and adapted by the storyteller set the story in his or her present context.

In the interpretation of myths, we must be careful to distinguish the type of myth we are talking about. Some myths address the cosmology of creation and the origins and history of a people. Some reveal lessons about ways to establish a better social order. Some describe the stages of physical, mental, and emotional development through the life cycle. And many others describe and prescribe a process for relating to the sacred, to the world of the divine beyond ordinary perceptions and habits. Finally, some myths combine elements of two or more of these purposes.

You can recognize a story as mythological when you perceive that it has happened to you in some form. In a sense, myths invite you to realize that you are hearing your own story. In myths, you must be willing to be transported into a world of imagination, reflection, and inspiration. They provide an ecological description of the powerful dynamics within you and reinforce the need to work with all these enlivening, if sometimes overwhelming and confusing, qualities and tendencies.

A sacred myth requires a redefinition of the world, an altered sense, not only of images and events, but of the spirit that animates them and of the sensibilities we bring to investing them with meaning. Myths give us mental and emotional access to some of the basic principles of spiritual growth presented in familiar language and structure.

Every mythological image in the story of Eros and Psyche carries a long history of usage and symbolism that was alive for listeners in the second century and still has vitality today. The story resonates, not only because we can see ourselves in the characters and plot, but also because the world and characters carry an historical significance that resides in us as recipients of a cultural legacy.

The Main Characters

In teaching stories of this type, we must extract the important lessons from symbolic levels of meaning, because they are rarely stated. In the myth of Eros and Psyche, the understructure reveals an entire model of spiritual alchemy that includes entering the unknown marriage, meeting the challenges of loss, separating illusions from reality, gaining inspiration, tapping the vital energies of life and of the sacred, confronting the world of the dead, healing from wounds, awakening through love, entering the heavens, and giving birth to a quality of sacred value. We explore these lessons through the actions of the characters themselves.

Eros

Eros is Love and is sometimes called the father of all, including Zeus and Aphrodite. Sometimes he represents a face of Zeus; sometimes Zeus is a face of Eros. Sometimes Eros is the son of Aphrodite and grandson of Zeus; sometimes they are all considered the same god. Through time, they are all reincarnated as father-son, son-father, father-daughter, mother-son—all moving in a dance of creation, family, love, and the drama of the unfolding story of life and relationships.

As both a creative and connective principle, Eros, for the ancient Greeks, played a critical role in the formation of the universe and its unpredictability.[1] Eros, as the connective element, included everything within the all-encompassing field of relationship. Without the power of inclusion, conflict and confusion can tear the universe apart. Open space and relationship can include all tensions and unpredictability.

Eros connects us to things beyond ourselves, beyond our vain self-preoccupations. The powers of Eros move the world as a primal creative and bonding force, as the heart-grabbing dynamic of Love, as the fire of passion, and as the impulse of desire, particularly sexual desire. Eros, as sexual desire, is a form of Love that is generative and connective. His story integrates the interpersonal and sexual faces of his divine force. He provides the juice—the semen—that impregnates experience, which in turn gives birth to meaning. Events are transformed into the conscious experience of aliveness and meaning by the thrust of Eros.

In the story, Eros must go through a series of tests and critical processes in order to mature as a loving force. Aphrodite sets him up with Psyche and he is subjected to his own powers of desire and love. He is wounded and must heal. He experiences loss, longing, and grief. He is trained by Sobriety in the retreat of his room in Aphrodite's house. Sobriety encompasses the qualities of virtue, clear-mindedness, and discipline beyond addiction. She is desire rechanneled.

Eros, as the wisdom of Love, learns to see the plight of Psyche. He reveals the power of Love to gather elements together despite the uncontrolled force of Love to disintegrate, to make things fall apart. By using the power of Love to awaken, rather than simply entrance, Psyche, he makes it possible for her to ascend to a divine level of being. He learns to reach out and help, revealing the nourishing and compassionate qualities essential to being a parent. He becomes a visible partner in the marriage and a welcomed member of the community.

At the beginning of the story, Eros manifests the bonding quality of Love, but with a chaotic intensity that threatens the order of the universe. In his marriage to Psyche, he becomes somewhat domesticated and is brought into the service of the spiritual. His story, one of primal passion and the vital energy of the heart, is partly about the process of giving form—the marriage and child—to energy as passionate love that has the potential for embodiment as mature love and compassion.

Eros also represents your special passion, your calling in the world, that which fires your imagination and inspires you to make your unique contribution.[2] In biblical mythology, this is called your spark or light, or more accurately the "Candle of God" that burns in you and shines through you. It is your mission in life that infuses everything with meaning and generates possibilities for creating benefit.

Psyche

For the ancient Greeks, all living things, including plants and animals, have, by definition, a psyche. Thus, Psyche is the principle of life, or the Life Force. As such, she is the power that animates the world.

Psyche is also the principle of individuality for living things, that which makes each particular thing unique within its own species. For Plato, Psyche is aliveness and a spiritual substance. For Aristotle, the phenomena of Psyche includes the capabilities for growth, reproduction, perception, thought, and personal action. For human beings, this includes the capacity to learn, a process that is essential for survival and growth—the embodiment of the principle I refer to as personal soul, or learning being. It is the personal soul that constructs a *persona* of personal meanings and identities that connects us to a dimension of life beyond the material world.[3]

The spiritual task we are given as a manifestation of the Life Force is to mature our personal soul as a learning being into a Sacred Soul as a conscious, divine presence. This divine potential is suggested in the myth by the reference to Psyche as a dewdrop of Heaven touching the Earth. It is also implied by another meaning of the word "psyche," butterfly. A mature butterfly is the result of a metamorphosis from one form into another.

The task of transformation in this story involves that part of us that has solidified meanings and identities into a personality. Thus, the body of Psyche refers, not so much to our physical form, but to our body of life experience, learnings and habits, emotional capacity, and imagination. For Psyche, the process of development brings the learning being into a wisdom being.

In accepting this challenging course of growth, Psyche is receptive, not passive. She opens to what arises and makes efforts only as needed to create the conditions for the natural forces and wisdom qualities to emerge. She does not initially have the capacity to behold all of Eros. Her personal soul must build a container, a Sacred Soul, by separating from the familiar—grieving, disintegrating, seeking, sorting, being inspired, dealing with pain, facing death, and awakening to divine love.

Aphrodite

Aphrodite, as a Great Mother Goddess of Love, Marriage, Sexuality, and Childbirth, is a Greek incarnation of the Egyptian goddess Isis, who was called Venus by the Romans. In this story, the true role of Aphrodite in the embodiment of spiritual wisdom is the most difficult to tease out. Her reaction to Psyche, the seductive way she gets Eros to do her bidding, her withdrawal from the world, her apparent rage at the marriage, and her unforgiving assignment of tasks for Psyche to perform can mislead and confuse us as to her role as the central wisdom figure in the story.

When we use mythological interpretations of the Olympian divinities of Zeus, Aphrodite, and Eros, we must distinguish the symbolic from the literal. Incest, for example, in the context of the gods, is different than it is in a human context. The gods are creative potentials, impulses and energies, and often the possessors of wisdom qualities. These forces and qualities make up one divinity, the One true nature that manifests in multiple dimensions and many ways. Each god represents a quality of the One and each is related to, and implicitly contains, all the others. Each provides a perspective on the others. Knowing one god intimately is to relate to them all. In the depiction of the sacred dimension, the union of sibling wisdom qualities flows naturally from the inner experience of sacred practitioners.

Even the question of who gives birth to whom depends on the context, both historically and spiritually. Historically, it depends on the politics of religious leadership, in which one group that follows a particular god in the family of gods gains ascendancy and promotes that god in the hierarchy of the family as either the original source of the others or the culmination of the evolution of the cosmic dynamics.

In our religiously judgmental and psychological culture, we often mistake the superficial description of motives for the meat of the lesson. We often think motive is more important than action or the results of behavior. In myth and storytelling, the motive is often simply a device to move the story along in a way that will keep the audience engaged. The motive as device will change according to the audience, while the structure and substance of the story will remain the same. It strikes me as strange that many analysts in the field of psychology, which looks beyond the surface layers of emotional reaction to underlying dynamics, themes, history, and belief structures, have tended to analyze this myth in ways that take the motivations as givens and the reactions as substance.

We must also dive beneath the surface to uncover the truth behind the apparent motivations and emotions of the gods. The angry, even hysterical reactions of Aphrodite to Psyche, as well as her outraged response to the relationship of Eros and Psyche, can be seen in a number of ways. For Apuleius, in the context of a Roman novel, it may have been a way of engaging his audience as well as mocking the ancient conceptions of gods, even as he is revealing their power and leading the reader toward an initiation into the worship of Isis, his chosen deity. In this sense, this also represents the political passing of an old sacred order for a new one more attuned to the sensibilities of Rome at a time when Christianity was struggling to emerge.

Yet even here, Aphrodite, as a form of Isis, is the guiding force through which Psyche grows, even if she appears so unpleasant and angry in dealing with Psyche that we may not want to give her credit or acknowledge her wisdom. Aphrodite's anger has the same effect as that of the wrathful deities of the Tibetan traditions. Their wrath is not an emotional reaction. In fact, it is meant as a tool for waking us up from our confusion. It startles us into paying conscious and precise attention to what will move us from our ordinary reactive trances to a more awakened sacred consciousness.

Moreover, in this Latin version of what was probably an ancient folk myth, Aphrodite plays the critical role of guide and master of initiation for Psyche and sets up the conditions that eventually lead to a marriage between equals. In placing Psyche in her service, Aphrodite creates her own dependency on the tasks being accomplished—sorting the grains of Aphrodite's household, bringing golden fleece to be used in the making of her fabrics, filling an urn with the precious waters from the river of life and death where even the gods hesitate to go, and finally bringing qualities of beauty from the world of the dead in order to celebrate the marriage of the Life Force with Love. Aphrodite also places Eros in a position where he must outgrow his old chaotic habits, not only to heal from the inevitable wounds that resulted from his wild yet hidden nature, but also to qualify himself for the marriage that he wants with the Life Force.

How often have you been confronted by the stern leadership of a parent/mentor who demanded that you qualify yourself by your clarity, your discipline, your actions, your wisdom, and your learning in order to be included in select company? And if you have not had such guidance, how deprived of confidence and competence are you? Whether you are given everything and have a sense of entitlement, or you are essentially ignored and have a sense of unworthiness, without real mentoring you may be haunted by feelings of helplessness.

Fathers of Eros

Eros has two fathers, Hephaestus (the Smith-God of Fire and the Magic of the Forge) and Zeus (the Monarch of the Heavens). Hephaestus was married to Aphrodite and some say Eros is the son of this union. The fact that Apuleius names Hephaestus as the father and has him appear at the final heavenly wedding makes a clear reference to the transformative arts. Hephaestus is often referred to as an originator of alchemy. He is also the maker of locks and keys, thus protecting secrets from intruders and offering the keys to those who qualify. Zeus, sometimes referred to as "step-father" and other times as simply "father," represents both supreme wisdom and the monarch of divine order, the "head" of the Heavens who confirms the sacred marriage.

Mythologically, the story reveals the path of psycho-spiritual development into sacred wisdom. The myth affirms the solidarity of the gods—of the sacred—with life on Earth, and particularly human life. Among its many levels of meaning, it also reveals alchemical symbolism, perspectives, and processes as part of the initiation and transformation into sacred consciousness. These alchemical dimensions are discussed at length in the chapters that follow.

Chapter Six

ALCHEMICAL PERSPECTIVES

Alchemical sublimation is freeing the energy of passion for transformation, expressing it, and then spiritizing it.

DENNIS WILLIAM HAUCK

The origins of alchemy in Western culture are generally traced back to around 300 B.C.E. in the area of Alexandria and North Africa, where Hellenistic Greek culture held great influence. Alchemy found its way into the science and spiritual practices of the Greco-Egyptian and Hebraic cultures here and was handed down primarily through the oral tradition and in writings that generally embedded the teachings in hidden codes and symbols.

In the fourth and third centuries B.C.E., Alexandria became a center for commerce, learning, and the Egyptian, Greek, and Hebrew wisdom traditions. Its influence spread throughout North Africa and the Mediterranean. For nearly a thousand years, until the Christian purges in the seventh century C.E. when all the libraries were burned and the teachers killed or driven into exile, this center of culture, philosophy, science, and art attracted seekers and teachers from all over the Western world. Alchemy traces many of its Western roots to the earliest periods in Alexandria and other centers in North Africa.

In the West, while the art and science of alchemy had been passed down since before 300 B.C.E.., the first use of the noun "alchemy" to describe this field of endeavor appeared in the writings of Zosimos, who worked in Alexandria in the third century C.E.[1] Nonetheless, spiritual practices of inner transformation are found in the followers of Pythagoras centuries before this and had already existed in India and China for thousands of years.

"Alchemy" is an Arabic word derived from *al* ("the") and *Khem* ("black land"), which referred to the ancient name for the Nile valley.[2] To the practitioners around the time of Apuleius, alchemy was concerned with the hidden properties and essences of the natural and sacred world and comprised the esoteric teachings that were known in this region of Egypt.

The process of turning the lead of ordinary experience into the gold of wisdom was referred to by alchemists variously as the "opus," the "transformation," or the "metamorphosis." For the initiated, the Greek and Roman myths, as well as Ovid's *Metamorphoses* and much of the work of Homer, were considered consciously alchemical works. It was customary for the Greeks, Romans, and Egyptians to hand down the alchemical wisdom to succeeding generations in the form of myths, fables, and coded stories.

Apuleius was well educated in philosophy and inspired by Plato. In his day, alchemy, like all the sciences and arts, was conceived to be a part of philosophy, a discipline of the love of wisdom and a practical means toward the embodiment of wisdom presence.

Alchemy has been and is considered by its practitioners to be a system for perceiving nature, the human design, natural and sacred processes and relationships, the cosmos, and the nature of being itself. In its various forms, it has been a dynamic force in the explanations of the world and in the esoteric spiritual practices of many traditions. Its esoteric philosophy and cosmological teachings on the act of creation set forth a path of wisdom and the embodiment of the most profound sacred qualities. Its system recognized three primary divisions of reality: the spiritual world of the sacred mind, the mental world of everyday personality and acquired habits, and the physical world of human bodies that have the potential for spiritual embodiment.

One of the earliest figures in the alchemical tradition was reportedly Hermes Trismegistus. He was called thrice-great because he was king, philosopher, and priest, and therefore possessed the three aspects of wisdom of the whole world. He is considered by many in later periods to be the father of alchemy in the West. Often identified with Thoth, the Egyptian god of revelation and wisdom,[3] he is the purported author of the alchemical book of laws known as *The Emerald Tablet,* as well as other tracts such as *Hermetica,* his philosophical treatise concerning creation. These works were written down in Alexandria in the second and third centuries C.E., though he supposedly lived many centuries earlier.[4] These writings drew upon the same ideas and sources as those of Apuleius, and it is possible that the practices in the North African mystery school of Isis and Osiris were adapted and included in what became known as alchemy at about the same time.

For thousands of years, writings concerned with alchemy and the path of an initiate presented the teachings through metaphors, allegories, stories, and myths. One reason for this practice was the desire of the masters to hide alchemical truths from "foolish" dabblers and misguided or uncommitted experience-seekers. Thus the descriptions of processes and tasks were made deliberately obscure.

At the esoteric levels, the teachers and codifiers of mythological, mystical, and alchemical stories have always been misunderstood. But they expected to be misunderstood, especially by those who could not see the wholeness of life and did not bother to learn the completeness of their systems of growth and wisdom.

The use of symbolic language was also due to the fact that the deeper truths being revealed and discussed could only be indicated metaphorically. No literal description could hope to convey the vast and powerful meanings contained in the subject. In addition, the fluid, flexible, and multidimensional nature of the sacred eludes any attempt to define the dynamics and nature of the spiritual in terms of certainty and rigid equations. The multiplicity of images used to symbolize substances, vessels, and dynamics is meant to convey the fluid, changing, and transforming nature of reality.

Alchemy was often associated with the generation of wealth. It is useful to distinguish between the material alchemist who works to change common metals into more valuable substances, the mental alchemist who works with thoughts to reduce them to basic insights and clarity that will enhance understanding, and the spiritual alchemist who works to discover and gather the treasures that are stored in Heaven, namely the qualities and energies of wisdom. The spiritual alchemist works to be transformed into the embodiment of wisdom presence.

Spiritual alchemists use the experiences of life, including thoughts and feelings, as their unrefined materials. These are then purified to their basic qualities of awareness and energy. Perceiving the fundamentally open and interrelated nature of all experience and phenomena, they then harmonize these qualities internally and cultivate the profound wisdom that transcends time and space.

Alchemists do not see themselves as engaging in some unnatural process. To the contrary, they conceive that they are aligned with the most natural processes of the cosmos and of the human design. Their curiosity travels to the innermost core of the elements of human nature, as well as to the farthest reaches of the cosmos. Their concern is more metaphysical than physical, and they see the physical universe as giving visible guidance in understanding and relating to the qualities of the invisible spiritual.

One of the core principles of spiritual alchemy that is found in Kabbalah and many other mystical traditions states that the physical and spiritual worlds are mirrors of each other, that the macrocosm is reflected in the microcosm and vice versa. In alchemy, this is called the "Doctrine of Correspondences." The Doctrine of Correspondences puts forth that what is true in Heaven corresponds to what is true on Earth, and what is true on Earth is also true of Heaven. They do not consider life, at its essence, to be divisible into a physical reality divorced from a sacred reality. For them, the subtlest part of matter is soul. The subtlest part of soul is spirit. And the subtlest part of spirit is God, also referred to by many as *Nous*, the One Mind.

Alchemists see chaos as the formless, shapeless matter from which the world and the sacred dimensions of being arose. For them, the process of macrocosmic creation provides a blueprint for the creation of sacred wisdom in the microcosm of personal evolution. In alchemy, you work with the *massa confusa*, or raw material, that is a manifestation of the original chaos from which the entire cosmos was created. For followers of these mystical arts, all life was viewed as the result of the same principle that operates in sex. Cosmologically, sex is the union of the formless with the formative to create form—the union of the open with the impulse to manifest creates matter. Sex is the original creative act replicated over and over to generate the entire universe.

Sex, at the human level, besides its procreative functions, expresses itself as love, movement, passion, enthusiasm, and fire. Our spiritual task as an initiate is to transform this energy from its roots in impulses and desires into the most refined and profound dance of love. For alchemists, sex is a form of love that produces the living universe. Thus life depends on love, and a spiritual life depends on spiritual love. One of the keys to eternal life therefore resides in eternal love. In fact, for them, it is the spirit of the sacred that brings everything to real life, that conveys meaning, and that makes divine rapture possible.

This work is often referred to as the *Magnum Opus*, the Great Work, because it represents the culmination of conscious inner work that embodies profound wisdom and energy beyond the limitations of mundane time, space, and routines. This final, freshly radiant and open state is known as the Philosopher's Stone. In the myth of Eros and Psyche, it is also symbolized by the nectar of the gods that completes the initiation of the personal soul as a learning being into the sacred, the refinement of the spirit and of you as a listener into the luminous world of the Divine, embodied in your aliveness, clarity, and love. All reality, inner and outer, is transformed in this process, producing the blessed experience of rapture, heavenly pleasure.

Chapter Seven

THE ALCHEMY OF MEANING
AND INTIMACY

*Even raw and messy emotions are a form of light,
crackling, bursting with energy.*

CLARISSA PINKOLA ESTÉS

As a human being, we are blessed with the miracle of consciously connecting with the people and world around us. We do not simply absorb data. We are designed to have feelings about the information so that we can protect ourselves, give direction to our actions, grow intellectually, emotionally, and spiritually, and form intimate relationships. It is our capacity to have a feeling about something that gives us the power to make one thing more significant than another, to connect more with some people than others, and to choose directions for our actions.

The process of turning raw data into meaningful information and of assigning value to some things more than others is a fundamental alchemical cognitive phenomenon. The world simply presents itself to you. You transform some parts of it into a personal palace with pillars of meaning, windows of selective perception, inhabitants of relationships, and treasures of values. You give form to the chaos of life through your structure of meanings and understandings, create gods to be followed and worshipped through your values, and generate bonds through your caring, affections, and ties to other people. In other words, you set time in motion as you give birth to your personal history, a new and never-before-seen flower that takes its place among all the other flowers in the field of life.

From an elementary standpoint, Eros connects and Psyche animates to create matter—both the material world and things that "matter" in terms of meaning and significance. There is an every-day process of the alchemy of creation of meaning. From birth, we begin the process of receiving masses of information and have the task of organizing it into patterns that can be used for recognition in the future. This is called learning.[1]

Based on physical needs for food, elimination, touch, and comfort, and the emotional needs for connection, affection, and play, we, as infants, not only form patterns, but also make some of them more important than others. This significance is tied to our sense of survival and well-being. We feel better emotionally when the information in our world meets an important recognized pattern. This process of establishing meaning and value is our personal story of the origins of our personal universe, in which we create something of emotional value from the chaos of our impressions of living in the world.

This early alchemical act of creating meaning and value operates on the same principle that drives the alchemy of the sacred. The difference is only that we work consciously to create sacred value (gold) and that we have the additional task of retraining our habit body. Our reactive habit body is accustomed to turning everything, even gold, into the lead of ordinariness and distress. Our challenge is to transform this body into a vehicle for turning everything into the gold of spiritual value and the elixir of sacred delight, to remove the muck of reaction from the hidden diamond of natural awareness and energy.

In our world of remolded and trivialized language, we are given the impression that change can occur through redefinition and reframing. Language becomes a device for numbing our sensibilities rather than enlivening meaning, for excusing wrongdoing rather than clarifying value, for deceiving rather than revealing, for persuasion rather than exploration and discovery, and for the perpetration of falsehood rather than the explication of truth. Pretense stands in the place of authenticity and truth, proclaiming that all things are relative and that authenticity and truth do not exist except in confused and undisciplined minds.

The myth of Eros and Psyche points to the process of creating authentic, sacred value. Psyche, as the Life Force, has the capacity to animate everything in the physical world and, through marriage to Eros (the force of connection), everything in the world of meaning as well. This may be where the use of the term "soul" becomes most applicable to Psyche. This story chronicles Psyche's journey as lover of the world, a maker of meaning. Meaning is what animates the invisible world for humans. Psyche not only animates it, she carries the seed of meaning that gives another, more sacred, dimension to the everyday process of experience. The sacred meaning then both creates new experience and provides a container within which the new and old experiences can relate.

When we look at Psyche in this way, we recognize her to be a lover who seeks and marries the force of Love itself; we see her as the mother of meaning, the invisible yet vital substance upon which our mental, emotional, and spiritual well-being depends. Even though commercial interests and addictive consumer tendencies seem blind to the real nature of life, the Earth, and the sacred, the dynamic of Eros and Psyche is always present, even if hidden from view, ready to bring us to the edge of authentic meaning and actively engaged experience.

Our capacity for a personal soul is completely open to learning as we grow and develop in the world. That soul is a learning being that expresses a uniqueness of the personal and yet is malleable, shaped by experience, culture, examples of others, and whatever successfully seduces its interest. It is made up of three parts: imagination in the form of memory, story, beliefs, fantasy, fears, and hopes; habits of mind and body that make up everyday time; longings fed by the light and heat of our Sacred Soul and connection to the Divine Essence of all things.

Our personal soul as Life Force and learning being is closely connected to our body and to living in the world of "matter," with the support of the sacred energy and wisdom of the spirit. Because the soul likes to "flesh things out" and enjoys elaboration, it is naturally drawn to storytelling and imagery. Our soul feeds on the experiences of everyday life and loves to express itself in stories, poems, paintings, music, dance, and artistic endeavor of all kinds.

Initially, this temple of the personal soul is shaped and moved by the interplay of natural impulses to explore, learn, and survive, and the constant impressions of familial, community, and cultural information and routines. In the story of Eros and Psyche, this is the life of a princess that is both esteemed and fundamentally unsatisfying and incomplete. Because Psyche is made of water and untested, unfired clay (the dew of Heaven touching Earth), she conforms to the way of life of her parents and their kingdom. She obeys their wishes, passed on to her from what they perceive as the demands of the powers to which they are held accountable. As Psyche moves on her own, she leaves the world of her parents and develops in new ways that transcend familial limitations.

At one level of meaning, as someone attempting to live a more conscious life, you must take on the task assigned by Aphrodite and sort out the seeds of your confusion into their elementary forms. Once all the seeds have been separated, like letters in a printer's case, they must be reassembled to give meaning. Each encounter with death releases the seeds from their usual combinations—sometimes in joyous, often in despairing, ways. Only as a new vision and new sensibility emerges do they re-form to create new meaning and sacred truth.

The Emotional Crucible of Meaning

Emotions are a manifestation of our capacity to relate. They involve perception, recognition, meaning, expression, and connection. Through the activity of emotions, we are able to sense something is true; we connect our self-sense to our own physical and psychological states; we bond with others; we relate to the world, life, and the sacred.

I use the term "emotion" to include all basic feeling states about anything. This extends beyond the standard list of emotions like anger, fear, love, sadness, joy, and anxiety to such feelings as pleasure, pain, desire, longing, wonder, inspiration, curiosity, ease, and will. These feeling states are all part of our sensory system—a system that not only perceives, but establishes how we relate to what we perceive.

I use the term "sensation" to mean the perception and experience of stimuli, and the term "feelings" to refer to the experience in the body of a configuration of sensations. Emotions are experiences that link feelings in the body with thoughts. They allow us to connect with people, things, places, ideas, and events.

To connect with something is to make it relevant, to give it special significance. When we make something relevant, we raise it above other information or data. Emotions not only move energy within us, they move us into relationship, sometimes toward close associations, sometimes toward more distant connections. Our sense of value arises from emotions, because we care about something. It is our caring that gives things special meaning and energizes us around that significance. With some

85

things, we experience a great charge; with others, there is hardly a noticeable vibration.

Moving Toward Sacred Meaning

The word "relate" means to connect as well as to recount, to tell a story. The two meanings are relevant, in that we connect as people through a sense of meaning, and each meaning is a story of our relationship to the event, person, or object in our life.

It is the nature of being human to desire connection to what is sensed or known. The connection may take the form of like or dislike, significance or irrelevance, wanting or avoiding, love or fear. For the untrained and superficial body-mind, this desire is reactive and uncontrolled. When we have consciously trained our attention, the desire is like a team of horses pulling the sacred chariot of dedication to wisdom and the creation of benefit in the world.

In simple terms, we can identify two fundamental dimensions of being—the superficial and the sacred. The superficial constitutes the surface level of reactive, unconscious thoughts and feelings. The sacred becomes manifest when we experience being conscious of the vaster dimensions and greater forces that operate in the world and make up the authentic nature of life. At the sacred dimension of what can be called God or "Essence," pure being, all there is is is. Essence is both totally open and completely immanent in manifestation. In the dimensions of potential and actual manifestation, the sacred is totally relative, everything that is, is of everything else that is. Thich Nhat Hanh calls this "inter-being" or "interbeing."

While interbeing simply is, we are designed to actively relate, to create relevant connections that organize our sense of the world, direct our attention, and further our activities. Consciousness involves relating, connecting our own self-sense to something within the totality of reality or to the totality of all that is— supreme consciousness. We make the richness of reality manifest in our innermost world of experience and meaning through our conscious use of our mental and emotional capacities.

The key is to see the extraordinary in the ordinary, to invest events, objects, activities, people, and experiences with meaning from the very depths of your being. The only way to see in this way is gradually to learn how to care, how to create beauty from what is available to you, and how to take care of what you create.

As with larvae in a cocoon, you know the preciousness by what eventually emerges. You cannot learn about its value in beauty by breaking it open prematurely. You must let it emerge on its own, in its own time, in order to have the butterfly break its way out and take its place as an earthly creature that can soar to the heavens.

In everyday life, we tend to sprinkle the dust of ordinariness and routine and reaction on the world. Wisdom brings the sense of a powerful living presence to each moment. By meeting the world with our full aliveness, we enrich, not only our experience, but the world itself. This is what makes life rich, significant, and wondrous.

When we engage emotionally and spiritually in the world moment to moment, we taste the deliciousness of living life beyond the safety of our habits and reactions. We feed ourselves, our community, and the larger world with the beauty of our tears, our celebrations, our whole-hearted quest to create value. When we express not only a feeling, but a larger sense of life, we participate in the making of a world that encourages, supports, and expands life through time.

Our head bursts, our heart explodes into the universe, and the cells of our body send out and take in simultaneously the threads of bonding when we experience authentic intimacy. We turn ordinary images, touches, words, and interactions into the delightful dance of love and praise. Our emotional capacity makes it possible for the inner to connect deeply with the outer and for the outer to be experienced as an innermost part of our own being. To be intimate is to know and be known, not necessarily in terms of intellectual understanding, but in the sense of being touched in our core, where our self-sense meets another and experiences profound connection.

This harkens back to the meaning of the word "religion" (from *re-ligio*, "to join or bind together"). Religion is about relating and bonding to that which is ultimate (Essence, Supreme Being, Tao, the Divine) and to one another.

Praise and Grief

We learn to feel the sense of a heart connection in experiences of praise and grief. As Martín Prechtel points out, when we love the things we have, it is called praise; when we love what is lost, it is called grief. The act of praise, whether spoken or quietly, deeply felt, creates a vehicle through which our sense of value takes form in the world. Praising calls upon our skills of eloquence and elaboration, amplifying the feeling and securing the connection. In praise for others, we are nourished in our soul by our appreciation, gratitude, and delight.

In grief, a sibling of praise, we work to consciously hold and be nourished by the energies of pain along with praise. Our heart is broken by the pain and longing, opening us to the fullness and substance of our condition and that of others. We allow the aliveness of the pain to enrich our celebration of the one we have lost. Our broken heart then expands, not bounded by self-concern, indulgence, comfort, pleasure, and limiting beliefs. This open heart sees clearly the connections to others that already exist. We sense that our pain is part of a larger energy stream of the pain and strength of all people.

Loss and grief are critical catalysts for breaking down superficial attachments and unconscious habits. When we do not grieve over the losses and tragedies in our lives and our world, we, individually and collectively, are unable to grow fully into the more profound possibilities of our nature and to realize the power of sacred wisdom.

Unfinished grieving, like all incomplete experiences and actions that have been resisted and denied, forms homeless energies looking for a place to take root and a way to manifest. These are like hungry ghosts who try to satisfy their insatiable longing by eating the life from our work, our relationships, and our connections in the world. They may take the forms of habitual reactions, obsessions, compulsions, addictions, depression, alienation, or a haunting sense of neediness. These ghostly energies will devour our dearest relationships and corrupt our best intentions.

Our emotions open us to sacred possibilities, even as they threaten to sweep us away with their power. When emotions are in the service of wisdom and relationship, not habitual reaction, self-preoccupation, and expression, they serve as a bridge between our soul and our body-mind. The meaning, love, and compassion of an open heart and the alignment of all our dimensions of being—from our most material functioning, to our sense of self and connectedness, to the wisdom qualities and energies of our soul dimension, to pure being and Essence—open us to the source of all that is, evoke our basic wisdom nature, give us the confidence to show up, connect us with life and the world, and guide us in the exercise of our true growth and freedom.

Necessary Wounds, Loss, and Challenges

When Psyche pricks her finger, the arrow of love breaks the skin so that blood, the water of life, can be released and exposed to the outer elements of life. This necessary wounding bonds us to another. In many cultures, a bond of blood is made by cutting a hand or arm and co-mingling the blood. In these cultures, this bond is stronger and more sacred than the exchange of sexual fluids.

The myth of Eros and Psyche suggests that the initial close relationship with the source of Love goes through a number of stages.

The wind brings the sensation of love, the feeling of being swept away and carried to another realm. This being carried away toward Love is a death. In the story, Zephyr lays Psyche on a bed of moist and fragrant flowers, like a funeral bower, where she sleeps and then wakes feeling calm and refreshed.

In the initial rush of love, our world may feel alive and beautiful as long as the object of our love is around. In this stage, our outer lover evokes our inner lover. Over time, the initial infatuation fades and dissatisfactions creep into the relationship. Our infatuation has blinded us to the real identity of our lover and now we want to know more. Doubts come to haunt us. We lose the intensity of our inner loving feeling.

Ambivalences grow and we inadvertently wound our lover and feel wounded and confined by the agreements in the relationship that we made in the stage of infatuation. When Psyche takes up the sword, she intends to end the marriage to protect herself and her unborn child. Before she can realize that intention, she gets a good look at her husband and falls in love again in a deeper way. This happens even as her wounds result in the loss of her lover, whether this manifests as physical separation or simply a distancing in the relationship. Such loss and distance evokes an intense inner longing for the love bond and for our lover.

Wounds of loss and the pains of grief present powerful challenges. If you shrink from the suffering and withdraw into your reactive habits of mind and feeling, you risk becoming numb to life and shut off from the possibilities of authentic connection. On the other hand, when you allow the pain to open your heart and work to gain a greater understanding of yourself, your lover, and of life, you embark on a journey that leads to emotional growth and greater understanding. By taking on the tasks of conscious growth, you sense the nearness of the quality of love, even as you struggle to find it embodied externally. You eventually discover your capacity for love as an inner quality.

You may sometimes wonder if you will ever experience a true union with your lover. There are many periods of falling apart and reforming ourselves as part of the maturing process. We come to know that we can never go back to the blind love of the past and look forward to loving in a new way. We enter relationships more as an equal, knowing that love is a quality that we bring to the world. We become a loving presence that can meet the love in the world.

When we finally do have a reciprocally loving relationship, it often occurs when we have surrendered hope and it comes upon us by surprise. Now we can marry in a new way that is more open, mature, and confident.

From Sexual Alchemy to Sacred Realization

The multidimensional story of Eros and Psyche contains, in addition to the social and sacred aspects of the love story, strong suggestive sexual elements. Sexual energy is used at a psychological level to create relationship. At a spiritual level, the sexual energy is channeled into the creation of a bliss-wisdom body that issues from the union of Love and the Life Force.

In certain ways, the story itself is similar to the "dual cultivation" found in Taoist alchemy. The sexual alchemists in this system tap the mutual energies of their partners to achieve ever-more-intense inner orgasms and ever-greater refinement of the generative energies. These are then gathered and used to create a subtle energy body.

The hidden valley that shelters the beginning of the relationship of Eros and Psyche can represent what is called the "sexual palace." Both Western mystery cult sexual practices and Eastern sexual tantric practices involve forms of sexual alchemy. In the tantric view, sexual union represents the ecstatic bliss of wisdom, love, and compassion. The female partner is the embodiment of transcendental wisdom, her vagina being the home of pure bliss. The male partner symbolizes skillful action and undeniable radiance, his penis being the diamond hardness of profound truth. The mother-father union, by incorporating all polarities, reveals the harmonious, inclusive nature of all being.

In the experience of sexual tantra, whether done completely internally or with a partner, the mixing of the generative energies and the intensification of their vibration reach a point where practitioners transcend the sense of being confined to a physical body. At some points they become *androgyne*, both male and female, fully energized and completely open. They become the energy and the space in which the energy radiates in all directions. They seem to exist beyond time and space, boundlessly open and supremely radiant.

The myth of Eros and Psyche tells us that the marriage must move from the sexual palace of the genitals to the upper domain of the heart (Aphrodite's palace) and be affirmed by the head, Zeus, who verifies their place together in the heavenly nexus of the head and heart. This generates Rapture/Bliss.

Sex, as one of the great mysteries in life, has the fiery power to generate bliss and pain, love and obsession, creativity and reactivity. It plays with male and female energy currents and engages the entire physical and energetic body. To work consciously with these powerful forces, we must bring another power into play. Aphrodite trains Psyche in this power through her various tasks. Eros requires this power to heal under the guidance of Sobriety as Virtue. This power—integrated multiple attention—can harmonize the various longings, the competing energies, and the cycles of time. It allows us to hold a continuous vision of utilizing and transforming the energies of aliveness and creation into sacred service throughout sexual union. Enhancing our capacity for multiple attention is the key to spiritual orgasm, the spontaneous energetic union of the Life Force with Love, resulting in divine Rapture and the integration of all levels of being in an unfragmented Reality of pure Presence.

In this spiritualization of our body-mind, we set out to create an indestructible diamond body of wisdom. In this process, we transform sexual and emotional desires into the desire for sacred beauty. We consciously use our senses as a vehicle to transport us to the domain of wisdom. We love the sacred and are guided by its teachings. Our realization and embodiment of this diamond nature gives rise to the experience of supreme rapture.

In Eros and Psyche's story, spiritual work is not simply a personal process. In fact, it is in relationship and through community that they grow—particularly in patience, courage, generosity, and wisdom. The wisdom I refer to here is profound wisdom, which grows out of the impulse to live by the deeper, more sacred truths of life. It is that aspect of who we are that can connect us to larger meanings and community beyond self-preoccupation. Love and wisdom ensoul our body-mind with sacred energy and enable it to generate a rich universe of divine beauty.

Chapter Eight

SPIRITUAL ALCHEMY

*Unless you fall in love with meditation and approach it
with total enthusiasm, attachment, and longing, you
cannot enter the realm of Awareness.*

SWAMI LAKSHMANJOO

Contrary to many simplistic religious beliefs, the spiritual is not about moral judgment and condemnation. It is about healing and enriching the world and creating beauty. It builds on the past, improves the present, plants the seeds of a better future, and honors the sacred that is manifesting in all life. As a tale about love, desire, and aliveness, the myth of Eros and Psyche is about neither a hedonistic quest nor an ascetic spiritual path. It is about the alchemical path of turning everything into the gold of wisdom, the embodiment of that wisdom, and living life as a total person and member of a sacred community.

In the world of spiritual alchemy, everything, including science, is a path to God. Inner work and outer actions become a building process of a temple to the sacred (the holy). Alchemy refines and polishes emotions like hate and grief with love so they can be used in building a sacred inner temple to serve the temple of the world. The inner temple of gold, made up of heart postures, meanings, and rituals, is maintained by being rebuilt every day. It is not confined to one place or time as the material world is. It is portable and can be recreated at any time, in any place. In spiritual masters, this sacred temple is being recreated all the time in each and every moment.

In the beginning, Psyche, as the personal soul (Life Force and learning being) is deluded into believing or pretending she embodies sacred beauty, which is the province of Aphrodite. The Psyche part of us must be trained and prepared and initiated into the mysteries in order to attain its divine or sacred potential. In the pretense of being the divine Aphrodite and, later, in her perception that Aphrodite is her enemy, Psyche is in wrong relationship to wisdom and the sacred. In these early stages, she reacts from ordinary confusion, as opposed to the sacred wisdom she attains.

The inner secret meanings of the mythological reveal themselves only to those who qualify themselves by their commitment to sacred practice and their experience in working with tasks of spiritual growth. At one level, this story describes the dynamic forces and challenges of life that make up the perpetual process of personal evolution. When we open to the deeper possibilities of the story, we can relate to the teachings hidden in the layers of symbol and metaphor. These are presented in such a way that even the uninitiated reader or listener can intuit, experiencing being nourished by the substance of not-quite-conscious insights.

If we view this myth solely as an initiation story, we may think we are teasing out its meaning and participating in the lives of the characters. In some sense, however, the story begins to participate in us, illumining our way of seeing and shaping our inner responses to the course of life. And, if we are prepared, we become a vehicle for the story to play out to its glorious conclusion. From the point of view of spiritual work, our lives are an opportunity for the larger forces of the cosmos to find conscious expression and to be realized in their full potential. The sacred legacy lives through us as conscious listeners and practitioners and is enlarged and strengthened by our willingness to surrender to its continued unfolding.

The story also integrates us into the world of the sacred and the dynamic configurations that are the core of an invisible body that vitalizes the material world, yet resides just beyond its physical grasp. Our conscious participation more fully integrates us into the larger story of life and the subtle workings of the sacred order. As an initiation guide, the myth must not be analyzed in terms of everyday mind and ordinary life. In addition to describing universal principles of the creation of meaning and intimacy, its deeper thrust is aimed at dedicated disciples who seek to realize the highest potentialities in themselves.[1]

The story tells us that we must do conscious work, work in the service of wisdom (represented by Aphrodite, Zeus, and Hermes), to mature our love impulse and to shape and refine our vital essence. Without this work, the alchemical marriage, which brings forth profound meaning, deep intimacy, and true joy, cannot occur. This work can be creative through the arts, religious through meditation, prayer, and/or ritual practices, or excellence in engaging life in a fully attentive, wholehearted, and soulful way. If we shrink from this work and try to leave our Life Force and Love untrained, we give an opening to self-preoccupation, victimhood, addiction, neediness, numbness, and the sovereignty of fear, anger, sadness, and hatred. We then vainly attempt to connect through our walls of separation and are imprisoned by our reactive habits and our insatiable longings.

In the sacred traditions of spiritual mastery, qualification through work and experience opens up the secrets of the teachings. Membership in the peer group of accomplished practitioners arises from the simple recognition of an extraordinary quality of presence, wisdom, and experience. Service to the larger story of life pries open the personal locks on the door of the spiritual path. The path itself then challenges each of us to move beyond the slippery slopes of doubt, to navigate in the dark of the unknown, and to overcome the seeming impossibility of transformation of our habit body and the embodiment of wisdom.

When Eros awakens Psyche from deathly sleep, he does so, not as the immature lover who would keep his beloved hidden from the world and himself hidden from her, but as a full-bodied lover who is willing to be responsible and to engage the entire company of the heavens. He pleads his case that both he and Psyche have qualified themselves, not only for marriage, but for full recognition in the assembly of the sacred.

These matured lovers give birth to Rapture, even if this issue of their relationship was conceived originally in simple pleasure. Isn't this the way it often works with parents? A child may be conceived of the love-lust of the parents, yet in the process, the parents are transformed by the miracle of having created new life. Over time, they not only mature, but come to know an entirely new kind of love, a deeper level of bonding, and a wondrous type of joy. The child and the process of parenting call forth a new quality of life and an engagement in the larger story of the community and life itself.

PART THREE

Myth as Mentor

Chapter Nine

THE PATH OF WISDOM

Everything becomes Fire, and from Fire everything is born.

HERACLITUS (540–475 B.C.E.)

For the ancient Greeks and for spiritual practitioners of all mystery traditions, the subtle realm or sacred world is intimate with the physical world. Both are dimensions of being. While the physical is more obvious to the everyday senses, the sacred levels are accessed and experienced through rituals and meditations that activate conscious attention.

Beyond the general alchemical principle of turning the base metal of everyday experience into the gold of wisdom, the myth of Eros and Psyche also contains specific alchemical symbols, processes, and steps in its structure and characters. These references in the myth, as presented by Apuleius and as retold here, reveal an entire system of sacred alchemy as initiation.

The Elemental Qualities of Alchemy

The ancient Greek formulation of the composition of matter, discussed by Empedocles (492–432 B.C.E.), by Plato in *Timaeus* (c. 360 B.C.E.), and later by Aristotle (384–323 B.C.E.), posited four elements.[1] In this system, as elaborated by Aristotle and also by the alchemists of later periods who wrote in Latin, everything was created from one original substance, the *prima materia*. From this original Chaos arose the four elements of earth, air, fire, and water. These four elements are not the same as the physical forms we see as the material world, but are subtle qualities or principles that manifest in physical forms. Each of these elemental qualities has two of four fundamental properties of the elements: hot, dry, cold, and moist. In this system, earth is cold and dry, water is cold and moist, air is hot and moist, and fire is hot and dry. For alchemists, each element is transformable into the others. The transformation is possible because each element shares a property with another element: earth and water share coldness, water and air share moistness, air and fire share heat, and fire and earth share dryness.

As humans, we are made up of the elements, but also give off the elements from our bodies: breath is air, tears and blood are water, discharges are water and earth, and warmth is fire. Women are able to create all four elements in a new life.

Since all physical and subtle forms are made up of these elemental principles and properties, transmutation from one form to another is possible, both on the physical plane and in the subtle or sacred dimension.

The Spiritual Meaning of the Elements

All these elements and phenomena arise from the *prima materia*, first matter, the common source of all things on all levels. *Prima materia* is essentially beyond representation, although this does not stop us from trying to describe or represent it.

As depicted in the myth and mentioned earlier in this commentary, the incestuous relations of the gods derives from the view that all are believed to have arisen from the same formlessness, original first matter. Therefore, the fundamental forces and qualities represented by the gods are always part of the same family. In alchemy, the fact that participants in a union or marriage come from the same family underscores the fact that they share the same essential nature and common origin, even though they may appear different or even opposite.

From a psychological and spiritual point of view, the *prima materia* is the power of consciousness to take form, sometimes referred to as imagination. This capacity to assume any form is the basis of learning and cognition. I have called the aspect of being that embodies this capacity the personal soul or learning being.

As Dennis William Hauck says in his book, *The Emerald Tablet*:

> The alchemists believed that the common act of imagination was somehow connected to the transformation of matter. They suspected that the imagination, in all its chaotic forms—from the horrifying creatures of nightmares to the lofty visions of science—is at the heart of the First Matter. It is the imagination that we discard in our youth as having no value; it is the imagination that is familiar to all, both rich and poor; it is the imagination which is hidden and yet known to everyone; it is the imagination that is "a stone and no stone."[2]

He continues:

> What the alchemists called the First Matter was grounded in the pure image-making ability of our minds that knows no

bounds, that has no singular characteristic other than its ability to take on all characteristics. But by the term "imagination" they meant a special kind of mental imagery or visualization that is directly connected to the ground of reality. Imagination without that connection is simply fantasy.[3]

What Hauck calls true imagination, as "the fundamental morphable energy of pure consciousness," here is akin to what I call the personal soul as learning being.

From another point of view, the *prima materia* is pure being from which awareness and energy arise as aspects of its nature that give rise to form. Energy, as the first movement, is seen as planting the spirit seed (egg) in the womb of primal awareness. From this emerges radiant Eros as a creative, connective force that then gives rise to all forms. This first fire sheds the light of distinction and simultaneously bonds all things with its heat (love).

In spiritual alchemy, the earth element brings the ability to give divine service. Air represents the motility factor in alchemy and is said to bring about the fellowship of all life. Fire gives the mastery that brings the ability and capacity to manifest Divine Love. Fire plays a significant role in the critical stages of alchemical transformation. In fact, alchemy is sometimes referred to as the art of fire. For the conscious spiritual work of inner alchemy, the inner fire is found through deep and profound meditation. Eros is regarded as a god of fire, particularly the inner fire of the heart. Water provides the mastery that brings peace. It is heavy, yet motile and adaptable. It is sometimes associated with philosophical mercury in its essence and is known as the water of life that can dissolve away impurities, killing old forms, and then regenerate and revivify things in a new way.

The French philosopher Gaston Bachelard (1884–1962) described the elements in terms of how they show up in experience. "Earthly joy is riches and impediment. Aquatic joy is softness and repose; fiery pleasure is desire and love; airy delight is liberty and movement."[4]

In the myth, Eros (who carries a torch, whose arrows engender the fire of desire, and who is often referred to as a dragon) is associated with fire. Both Aphrodite (born from Ocean foam and using the Ocean as a place to retreat) and Psyche (whose birth is described as a dew drop from Heaven impregnating Earth) are connected to water, although Psyche is also associated with the Earth. Fire can be viewed as an active force, a radiant spirit. In some myths, fire is divine energy originating in Heaven and coming to Earth as lightning, or is stolen by humans from the gods. In other myths, fire originates from the sexual acts of the gods and represents intense passions such as love and hate. Water is seen as more adaptable, more akin to the openness of the learning aspect of the soul. In many sacred traditions, the meeting of fire and water is the original creative act.

Psyche's Tasks and the Elements

Psyche, having taken up residence in Aphrodite's home, the palace of the heart, and inspired by the distant presence of Eros (Love and desire), performs a set of tasks demanded by the great goddess of creation and love herself. The tasks that Aphrodite gives Psyche work with the principles of the elements and utilize their spiritual significance to shape the development of the personal soul.

The first task, sorting out the pile of seeds, involves pausing, mindfulness, and sorting, and Psyche uses the grounding forces of the ants of the earth to sort the various grains and seeds of thoughts and feelings that originate from her earthly experience.

The second task, obtaining the golden fleece, engages all four basic elements—earth (reed), air (wind), water (stream), and fire (rams and the Sun). The reed, as a musical instrument of the Earth that is activated by the wind, creates music that both calms Psyche and gives her instruction. The music focuses the mind to each note of its song. The song, as a sequence of notes of instruction, directs the mind on how to gather the fire (golden fleece) in amounts that can be used in weaving the fabric of meaning and wisdom. She is prepared for completing the task by combining earth, water, and air. In terms of the symbolism of the elements in the body, she uses the head (air) in combination with the abdomen (earth) and the sexual center (water) to approach the heart (fire) and its heat of transformation.

The third task involves retrieving water from the river Styx. This deals with the spacious motility of the air (the eagle of Zeus) and the creative fluidity of water (the river of life and death). This task requires the panoramic vision of awareness (Zeus as the head of consciousness) to gather precisely the essential, fluid energy of life to be carried in a crystal urn (earth) by Psyche to the home of the heart, the palace of Aphrodite.

The journey to the Underworld in the fourth task is guided by a tower of the palace of Aphrodite (towers in alchemy represent a furnace/fire). This task emphasizes going deep into the Earth, a kind of burial, crossing the river of death, and then ascending to Heaven before the final, greater marriage of Heaven and Earth represented by Eros and Psyche and the affirmation by Zeus and Aphrodite.

The Fifth Element

In completing the fourth task, Psyche dies to her old form. She is then reawakened by Eros, who now embodies love as a disciplined and inspiring force. Then a new element is introduced that is represented in three different forms: the nectar, the heavenly marriage itself, and the child that is born. Nectar is the gold of profound wisdom that is needed for the full transformation into the gold of Divine Wisdom—the Philosopher's Stone of immortality—and entrance into eternity. The marriage unites Heaven (Eros) and Earth (Psyche). It also weds the bonding force of Eros with the Life Force of Psyche, making the Life Force divine and the bonding manifest. The result is Rapture, a Divine Bliss that transcends any form of temporary sensory pleasure.

The new, or fifth, element results when the four fundamental elements are harmonized and reconciled in a unity. In the alchemical tradition, the Philosopher's Stone is often called gold and the Elixir, drinkable gold. The essence of the Elixir, the liquid gold, is the supreme Wisdom that is clear, indestructible, and made of the original nature of the world and all being. This element paradoxically arises from the alchemical process and yet is the natural state beyond all impurities and conflicts. It is the wisdom of salvation, enlightenment, the Tao, and the nature of mind that is beyond everything yet immanent in everything, that is always present but only realized and embodied through conscious spiritual work.

Gold is seen as the perfect immutable metal that withstands the forces of fire and water. Gold in the inner alchemical tradition is not the material gold, but the Wisdom of the Divine that resides in the heart. According to some, the heart is the sun of the microcosm that corresponds to the Sun of the macrocosm. In alchemy, the gold that can withstand the tests of fire is the embodiment of divine wisdom in a masterful and mature human being.

The Alchemical Sequence

Just as the elements were more principles for the Greek than substances, so the operations of alchemy are more descriptions of universal dynamics than specific chemical processes. These operations are generally viewed as part of the universal formula for a spiritual technology that had been passed down through generations from the times of the very ancient Greeks and Egyptians. These operations sometimes happen spontaneously, but generally require intentionality in their performance. They can be applied to the transformation of the physical, mental, and emotional bodies and to the cultivation of our spiritual nature.

In alchemy, there are generally three main classes of operations: purification, refinement, and generation. Each stage is represented by an animal. In the first stage (purification), a serpent or dragon appears as Eros, who is born of the "dragon breed." In the second (refinement), a lion or, as in this story, a ram appears. An eagle represents the third phase (generation).

These stages can be further elaborated as seven steps: calcination, dissolution, separation, conjunction, fermentation, distillation, and coagulation. These steps will be discussed in more detail in the chapters that follow, along with their specific applications to the myth of Psyche and Eros. However, a brief description of them at this point will give you a basic idea of the progression in the alchemy of spiritual transformation and initiation.

Calcination reduces a material to dust through the application of the heat of fire. This process converts our soul into a basic form that renders it more open so it can receive the influx of divine spirit. This is often seen as critical to an initial death process of our habit body.

Dissolution, also called *nigredo* and "putrefaction," is the second step in this initial death of our habit body, bringing down habits to more essential forms of the life process.[5]

Separation, the third step, divides thoughts from feelings to make their nature clearer, and distinguishes between the mundane and the sacred ways of being. During the process of separation, we gain understanding and the ability to discriminate between illusion and reality, superficial appearances and deeper truths, and conventional and profound wisdom. In this process, we discard unauthentic and unworthy thoughts, feelings, and behaviors or simply leave them behind. The process of separation clarifies the domains of our lives, the dimensions of our being and awareness, and points us in the direction of the sacred dimensions.

The inner alchemical process of separation also refers to a "death" to the world. The aim of this death, which separates us from the ordinary world (the world of reactive habits), is to free our soul from old attachments, fears, longings, and turmoil. After we make this transition, an inner equanimity emerges in us and our personal soul becomes conscious of its own true nature. It perceives the difference between habitual reactions that sow the seeds of future distress and sacred engagement that creates the conditions for greater awakening and wisdom.

In many alchemical systems, there are three deaths of separation. So it is with the story of Eros and Psyche. The first occurs when Psyche is carried from the cliff to the hidden valley, where she promptly goes to sleep (death to childhood and old family home). The second occurs when she throws herself in the river after Eros departs (death of old hopes and dreams). The last occurs when deathly sleep overcomes her on her return from the Underworld (death of remaining traces of old habits and karmic traces), before the reunion with Eros and final realization and embodiment. Marriage and the creation of a sacred child always involve a sacrifice or death. The death before the wedding indicates the extinction of the earlier habit body and sense of separation. This makes an opening for the new union and fresh engagement. Alchemical theory holds that new generation cannot take place unless preceded by a death.

Two other parts of the story suggest forms of death: the wound to Eros that forces him to separate from the world and from his old ways of capriciously pricking others with uncontrollable desire engendering undisciplined love, and Psyche's thought of suicide during the second task, which may represent the death of old motivation, clearing the way for the fire of the divine inspiration of the golden fleece.

The fourth step, conjunction, brings together two or more of the elements and often gathers opposites into the same space. This is also referred to as a wedding or marriage. In the process of alchemy, there are a number of dissolutions, separations, and conjunctions as the soul is matured by life and conscious work. Conjunction generates the space for all the fragmented elements of our soul to be brought together in a more harmonious space.

The three conjunctions of alchemy are presented in this story by the unions of Eros and Psyche. The first takes place in the hidden valley, which corresponds with the union of male and female seeds. The second takes place when, after the death of the soul, it is revived and united with the spirit of Heaven. This happens when Eros revives Psyche on her return from the Underworld. The third takes place in the highest Heaven and represents the final union that marks the realization and embodiment of Divine Love and Wisdom with the Sacred Soul.

In the fifth alchemical step, fermentation gives rise to something new and more sacred from the remains of the previous processes. The soul rises to a new level in this first part of the final phase of transcendence. Often, this involves the application of the heat of fire, usually from the Heavens, to raise the level of the entire process and prepare it for more complete transformation. In fermentation, our soul is reanimated and feels the fire of inspiration that nourishes growth and realization.

Distillation is the sixth step and a final refinement of the process. Distillation eliminates the remaining impurities so that the purified elements can come together again, after having been separated in the third step. This purification and clarification extracts the essence of experience and capabilities that are the foundation of wisdom and final transformation.

Coagulation, the last step, brings together all the elements in a final marriage that represents transformation and embodiment of Wisdom and the creation of the gold of Profound Wisdom, the Philosopher's Stone, the diamond of true clarity, and the Elixir of sacred creation in the dimension of the eternal. In this process, the wisdom energies of Heaven, of the sacred, are brought into the world as a new and refreshing presence that can be a benefit to all people.

One of the symbols for coagulation is the Philosopher's Stone. This relates to the idea that this state is the supreme crystallization in form of the invaluable life-essence. In Western alchemy, it is compared to such precious stones as the ruby, pearl, sapphire, and diamond. In Buddhist teachings, it is depicted as a diamond. A pure diamond is close to an absolutely clear physical substance and is the hardest, most indestructible thing in our universe.

The order of the steps of transformation is always presented in confusing ways by alchemical writers, who do not want to be too explicit. In addition, a great deal of overlap occurs among many of the steps. For example, the operations of calcination and dissolution often occur simultaneously. Both are forms of cleansing and purification. The fact that calcination is associated with fire and dissolution with water simply demonstrates a primary theme in alchemy, namely that opposites can work together and, in fact, must unite in the process of transformation. Our job as aspiring adepts is to provide a spacious container for these complex, competing, and paradoxical forces that operate in us and in the world.

The view that we must work to create a marriage of the Life Force with Love, of the material with the sacred, is based on the Hermetic assumption that we, as human beings, become divided within ourselves as well as separated from the sacred aspects of nature (and often the physical presence of nature). This split causes endless pain and needs to be reconciled. Further, the union of Heaven and Earth, of male and female forces, and of the elements produces a new substance, a new effect that heals the afflictions of our soul and generates divine rapture. This union combines our creative and connective powers with our capacity for learning and wisdom, and creates a child of pure love and sacred joy.

Alchemical Imagery and Symbols

The alchemical imagery in this myth weaves a colorful tapestry of the world of transformation. The rich images and lines of development reveal qualities of the sacred that inform our own relationship with the spiritual domain and with our own maturation as aspirants and servants of the Divine.

In alchemy, Psyche, usually called "soul" or "anima" in the literature, provides the raw material for the creation of the Philosopher's Stone, the gold of Wisdom. Her dissolution and separation are referred to as the death of the "body," which means the transformation of the personal soul as learning being and "habit body," as I have called it. Through her three deaths, the sacred aspects of her soul are released to go through various unions with the spirit, represented by Eros, leading to the alchemical wedding. In the course of putrefaction, our personal soul, as a container, is purified so that the personal and sacred aspects of our soul can be reunited in the divine marriage and the resulting wisdom qualities embodied in our lives.

For many alchemists, Eros, usually referred to as Cupid in the alchemical literature, is both the secret fire that dissolves the elements and reduces them to *prima materia* and the Love essence released by the Elixir, the Philosopher's Stone, the supreme sacred Wisdom. Robert Fludd, in *Truth's Golden Harrow*, called the Elixir the true temple of wisdom, the "impregnable castle of Cupid that powerful god of love."[6]

Eros is also associated with the bee and with honey. The sting of the bee and the arrow of Eros both signify the secret, sacred fire that breaks down metals and destroys the outmoded state of being. Eros is considered a dragon or winged serpent because of his power to wound with his arrows. These arrows break down our routines with the poison of love, which is also the sweet honey that can nourish our wisdom nature.

The role of Aphrodite in alchemy is complex. She can represent the chaotic initial state of the world, as in her associations with the Ocean. This can have connotations of primal nature. The sea or Ocean is often taken as a synonym for the *prima materia* from which the universe was created. In another sense, she can represent the chaos of our initial confused reactive state from which we must progress. This is evident in her emotional displays that hide her basic wisdom nature. More frequently, and especially in this story, she is the goddess of Love and the mother of Eros (and, in some sense, the mother of Psyche). In alchemy, it is in this capacity that she presides over the sexual union of the male and female seeds in the alchemical wedding. She is the governess of the process of union that creates the Elixir, the Sacred Wisdom.

In the story, Aphrodite is the one who introduces Eros to Psyche and thus sets up their initial union. She withdraws from the scene, so they go through this initial meeting themselves. With the separation that happens after this initial union, she is the one who takes care of Eros and sends Sobriety to supervise his recovery. She then sends for Psyche through the god of communication and transformation, Hermes. In this way, Aphrodite brings both Eros and Psyche under the roof of Divine Love, which is the home in the heart. She gives Psyche four tasks. Having prepared Psyche and Eros, she then lets them reunite for their second union. And finally, she dances at the divine wedding, which represents their third and final union in the sacred.

Apollo is the Sun and also represents gold. It is the oracle of Apollo that sets out the initial instructions to the father of Psyche that begin the journey and explicitly state that a marriage must take place. This, along with the references to the dragon and death, indicates that this story is about the path of alchemical transformation.

Hermes represents the universal agent of transformation. In alchemy, Hermes, usually called Mercurius (or Mercury), is frequently described as the water that does not wet, or as water and fire. He represents communication between the domains or dimensions of being and the movement between them. In the metaphysical alchemical tradition, Hermes carries the divine love essence that kills illusion and pretension and permits truth and wisdom to arise.

He also represents both a unity around which opposites come together, as in the serpents on his caduceus, and a medium of unity that calls forth the alchemical wedding.

The caduceus, the wand of Hermes, with two intertwining serpents crossing each other to form three circles, symbolizes the dynamic circulation of fundamental male and female energies and the three separations and unions that are part of the alchemical work in creating the sacred marriage. This healing and awakening rod has the power to reconcile conflicting elements and forces into a more inclusive harmonious state and to support the transition of the soul into the domains of sacred wisdom. In physical terms within the human body, the shaft of this staff represents the spinal cord (the central axis of the nervous system and the path that generative sexual energy takes to the higher centers of the heart and the head). The movement of these energies to the higher planes is called, in some alchemical literature, the "Hermetick Raptures."

Another clue to the alchemical sources of this story for Apuleius is that Hephaestus (Vulcan) is presented as one of the two fathers of Eros and the former husband of Aphrodite. He cooks the meal for the final wedding in Heaven (the divine, alchemical marriage). Hephaestus works with fire and symbolizes the archetypal alchemist. Mythologically, he is often viewed as the founder of alchemy. He is also referred to as the secret fire of the alchemical work and as the midwife for the birth of the Philosopher's Stone.

The terms Heaven and Earth also refer to states in the stages of the refinement of matter, of soul, in the alchemical process. When our condition is gross, Earth prevails. When we have been refined to the levels of subtle energy and wisdom, we gather the fruits of Heaven. Then we can bring the qualities of Heaven to Earth to transform our ordinary life on Earth into a sacred temple of Heaven and manifest Wisdom Presence in our life. At this point, Earth represents embodiment.

The Earth also represents conjunction and is considered the mother of life on the planet. In this sense, Psyche represents Earth that is seeking union with Heaven in order to create something extra. From the point of view of ancient agriculture, Psyche is the living presence of Earth and Eros is the cultivator that planted and plowed her fields through the sexual act. At the physical level, they generate more life. At the level of the sacred, the point is not to create more life, but to intensify the experience of life. That intensity is the fully conscious aliveness that radiates a loving connected presence.

The tower of the palace of Aphrodite represents the furnace or *athanor*. The furnace of the heart in mental and spiritual alchemy raises the temperature of our attitudes in order to increase the vibration of our thoughts. Our inner attitude, what is here called our "heart posture," determines and regulates the feelings that are tied to our thoughts. The heart postures of openness and witnessing allow our thoughts to settle into their own nature, creating a sense of equilibrium and peace. The heart postures of aspiration and dedication create the will for conscious work that is necessary to outgrow old patterns and cultivate wisdom.

No emotion raises the vibratory level of the heart as a furnace of transformation as much as unselfish love. Any sublime love that carries you beyond self-concern has this sacred power. Your love as a parent, as a partner in a love relationship, and as a caring person performing loving service for those in need can all have this unselfish and exalted quality. Your love for the sacred, combined with devotion to making the divine manifest through you, provides you, as a spiritual alchemist, with the most powerful furnace.

In terms of the tasks that Psyche performs, some additional qualities can be added to the alchemical imagery already discussed. The first task (sorting the seeds) clarifies the personal soul. The second (obtaining the golden fleece) gathers sacred inspiration and direction. The golden fleece is a form of Divine Wisdom that is used to catalyze the alchemical process. In alchemy, some gold is needed to harmonize and create gold from the four fundamental elements of earth, air, fire, and water. The acquisition of the golden fleece is considered dangerous work that requires courage and skill so as not to be overwhelmed by the radiance and heat associated with the rams.

The third task (retrieving sacred water from the river of life and death) draws up the vital, sexual, generative energies of life using the mind, represented by the eagle of Zeus and motivated by connections to Love (Eros), and draws these energies into the heart center, the palace of Aphrodite. The final task (journeying to the Underworld) is a dark retreat where, stripped of all familiar objects of the everyday world, we must deal with primal darkness. In the course of this work, all remaining traces of our past habits are removed, making us ready to bring back to our heart the inner radiance that has become evident in the dark.

In alchemy, during the process of distillation and death in the journey to and from Hades, the vessel carrying this force is often portrayed as a coffin or casket. This vessel is often referred to as the womb. This womb is also called a cauldron where inner fire heats inner drops of consciousness, distilling them into essence drops of pure awareness, energy, and being. In some systems, this cauldron is located in the abdomen, in others, in the heart. This Hellenistic story seems to suggest the womb is the heart in the home of Aphrodite.

According to Dennis William Hauck, in the ancient alchemical writing of *The Emerald Tablet* that he says was housed in the Library at Alexandria, it is stated:

Separate the Earth from Fire,
the Subtle from the Gross,
gently and with great Ingenuity.
It rises from Earth to Heaven
and descends again to Earth,

thereby combining within Itself
the powers of both the Above and the Below.[7]

The "Above" refers to the sacred dimension in which everything exists in a state of potentiality. This is the formative. The infusion of energy from "the Above" can take many forms, such as mystical experience, a sacred vision, a near-death experience, a perceived moment of divine grace, or simply beholding beauty. The conditions for this breakthrough are set up through meditation, intense prayer, participation in sacred ritual, and/or a retreat under the guidance of an authentic teacher.

As mentioned previously, the supreme wisdom that turns the lead of everyday experience into the gold of Wisdom and sacred devotion is represented by the divine nectar. This divine state is also referred to as an Elixir, daughter, the Philosopher's Stone, a rose, a lily, a lotus blossom, and a bird.

Using the Alchemical Path

In the process of spiritual growth, our simplistic relationship to what is divine is replaced by a more mysterious, multifaceted, and imaginative connection. A world is destroyed and replaced by another that has the potential for beauty, even as it confronts us with disorientation, pain, and challenge. We cannot make the experiences of bliss and divine connection happen; they are gifts. Yet our efforts create the conditions that give such gifts a chance to be received and the sensibilities of how to open the gifts when they arrive.

In spiritual alchemy, you must penetrate thoughts, feelings, and attitudes to their spiritual core with a force that overcomes their reactivity and apparent validity. This force resides in the power of conscious attention.

The heart posture of spiritual alchemy involves a very special kind of perception of reality that embraces all of life, recognizing the inherent interbeing and unity of all things. It relates to all reality with a sense of presence and to the divine nature of reality with openness and wonder. Your soul is moved by an insatiable longing for spiritual maturity and growth, and by pure love for creation and wisdom. It is also motivated by the vital importance of being a beneficial presence and contributing something of value to human evolution and life itself. Increasingly, your desire for the wisdom that unites all dimensions of being grows, so that the radiance of the sacred can illumine your sensory, material world. When spiritual awareness is united with your body freed from reactive habits, sacred knowledge and consciousness can be put into action, made manifest in the phenomenal world.

The light of consciousness has both an awareness aspect and an energetic quality. As awareness, this light is a clarity that reveals hidden patterns and peels away layers of confusion and rigidity to uncover the underlying qualities of life and Wisdom. As energy, it activates the circulation of qualities within our body and between our body and our environment. We can then balance and reconfigure the circulation of the various energies and combine them in unions that create new, more subtle qualities that eventually are collected in a womb to give birth to a sacred energy body of light.

According to alchemy, in both its physical and spiritual forms, the transformative Elixir cannot arise or the transformations take place without the material of the process first being dissolved into its primary nature. For the human soul, being dissolved into its primary nature means releasing reactive habits of body and mind and resolving or making peace with inner conflicts. When our soul is sufficiently refined, the qualities and energies of the sacred can enliven and bring radiance to it and create the possibility of a freer, more sacred, state of being.

Chapter Ten

IN SEARCH OF AUTHENTICITY

The most profound experience of life is our dealing with loss.
Accepting loss. And continuing life after the event has happened.
This is a most normal thing, an instinct we all have. Somehow to
repair whatever was destroyed and, if possible to bring it back. Now
it is impossible to bring it back. But there is a very, very important
element in this effort to make this reparation, to make this tikkun,
which is what I think unites people, makes it possible for people to
communicate, and to be open to each other. To be generous.

SAMUEL BAK

Why is it such a tragedy for Psyche to be unwed? The meaning here has to do with the sense of isolation and alienation from the sacred. Psyche, in the midst of admiration, is not connected to the ongoing life of the community and to creating a viable future because she is cut off from the gods. She is living a pretentious, unauthentic life.

Beauty is also a transformational reference in this mythological story. The story makes the distinction between pretentious and sacred beauty. Relating to beauty superficially leads to self-preoccupation and the trivialization of beauty as vanity. The sacred way of connecting to beauty involves having physical beauty evoke the greater and wondrous invisible beauty.

Life itself demands more than surviving in the familial house. Psyche, as Life Force and personal soul, knows she must move on to the unknown marriage and an encounter with death. She realizes that the true cause for mourning is the time she spent pretending to sacred beauty and divine qualities, for this illusion was a form of death in which true aliveness and authenticity were neglected in the preoccupation with appearance over substance. She knows that life will shrivel and wither if confined to the surface skin without nourishing the organs that give the body substance. She knows that the kingdom will continue to be devastated by drought from the absence of the true goddess unless she turns her life over to the forces of the sacred. When Aphrodite, goddess of fertility, creation, and beauty, recedes from the scene, the world becomes desolate.

Psyche yearns for the marriage, the connection that lies beyond the house of her parents, beyond the realm of the familiar. This longing is more than Psyche's; it is the longing of the story to move beyond the mundane into the treacherous waters of passage and gain confidence through things that matter (experiences that can mother a new growth).

We get a sense of Psyche's basic intelligence and insight when she reveals to her parents that she is "as if dead" when people worship her image rather than honoring the real Aphrodite, when they don't see who and what she really is. She accepts the marriage/death that will take her beyond this lonely, barren place where the depths are ignored and the surfaces occupy the attention.

It is from the divine dimension that the fire of Love comes to Earth as Eros to court and love the malleable watery clay of the personal soul, Psyche, who is ready to leave the familiar and, however reluctantly and anxiously, encounter the unknown that will give her life substance and meaning.

Purifying the Reactive Habit Body

Calcination is the process of reducing a substance, in this case our everyday assumptions, beliefs, fears, and longings, to ashes. Psychologically, the calcination stage is also known as the "death of the profane." During this phase, the routine identities and habits of our mind and body are undermined and our world is shaken to its core. The basic issue with mundane life is that our rigid identities, reactive habits and feelings, and material concerns receive our attention and life energy rather than our development in and contributions to the sacred.

In alchemy, the first application of fire in the process of calcination reduces the substance of these habits to cinders. Here, we are burning off the surface layers of our personality to reveal more of our essence, our *prima materia*. In order to grow, our soul must first become openly exposed through the painful process of calcination, in which we lose our routine, habitual identity, and our reactive connections to the everyday world.

The light of fiery consciousness, applied to our habit body, is intensified by the desire to live authentically and with integrity. Ignoring our impulses for an authentic life often leads to spontaneous explosions of the emotional, highly reactive garbage that we carry in our bodies. But remember that it is disintegration that lets something fresh grow. This disintegration most often occurs naturally in the course of our lives through what Hamlet called the "slings and arrows of outrageous fortune." This process can also be instigated intentionally as part of a spiritual path through practices of reflection, mindfulness meditation, and renunciation.

Within every spiritual discipline, there are methods taught to students that consciously create the conditions for this burning of mental/emotional constructs and the initial glimpse of true essence. In the Eastern traditions, these constructs are called *karma*. Karma refers to actions and their results. Every experience and behavior leaves "traces" or "impressions" on us and on our environment. These footprints are karma; taken together, they create a body of karma. Karma, in this sense, is the reactive habit body of memory, personality, preferences, likes and dislikes, beliefs and belief systems, dreams and systems of perception, emotional, psychological, and religious conditioning.

The myth of Eros and Psyche moves continually toward the eternal, the domain of the sacred that is beyond the surface level of problems and reactions. At each stage, the process is intensified, so that we can burn away and digest the unassimilated thought patterns, habits, fears, longings, and psychological complexes that drain our life energy and block the flow of sacred energy within us and from us to others.

Dissolution is a further breaking down of our hopes, fears, doubts, expectations, and assumptions about the world. This phase works particularly on the emotional habits that keep us from experiencing our true nature, our radiant essence. During dissolution, it is common for previously unconscious and often unknown mental and emotional material to surface into consciousness.

Water is associated with dissolution. Initiation rites of immersion and baptism cleanse and dissolve old ideas and habits and make initiates more fluid and adaptable to new possibilities. Water is symbolic of the capacity of matter to change. This primal capacity for change is considered an aspect of the chaotic *prima materia*.

Only by totally dissolving can a new, more spiritual form arise that is eternal. We must die to attain the immortality of the sacred. In the story of Eros and Psyche, dissolution occurs three times, in images of bathing, tears, and streams. The baths that Psyche takes when she arrives at the hidden palace wash away the fears and assumptions that she brought from her parents' house. Then she immerses herself in the stream as part of her first death attempt after Eros has disappeared. This dissolves the assumptions and habits that she formed in the naïvely happy phase of the relationship and exposes a core fear and despair, as well as her deep longing for her husband. The third dissolution is embedded in her desperation about getting the golden fleece from the fiery rams. Here, she cleanses herself of the immature ways of thinking that tend to polarize everything into extremes. In this process, a more nuanced way of perceiving arises and she realizes that she does not need to kill herself or the rams. She only needs a small amount of that fiery passion and inspiration to fulfill her task and learn her lesson.

Air also plays a role in this process of purification. Zephyr, the West Wind, is associated with mercurial vapor and plays a role in the clarification process. Thus Zephyr supports the initial purifying of Psyche by bringing her into the palace of Eros for their initial union, carries the sisters (doubts) to the palace, and withdraws from the sisters of doubt when their deaths are necessary for the process of further clarification before the next stage can begin.

The Moon and Sun of Change

The suggestion, early in the story, that Psyche is really the result of celestial dew, which has the magical and healing qualities of the sacred, indicates that the Earth or the body is about to be cleansed and reanimated. Since dew is symbolically associated with the Moon, it also indicates that Psyche is somehow related to the Moon, perhaps even a child of it. In earlier times, the Moon represented a cool, reflective, calm, and changing quality that went through cycles associated with feminine sexuality. Mythologically, the water of the Moon is considered the dewdrops that appear on the Earth at night.

The Moon is also associated with death and rebirth, or resurrection. For three nights, it disappears and then returns to grow through its stages again. Unlike the Sun, which is resurrected daily, full blown, the Moon has cycles that are longer and must go through stages of increase and decrease just as we do. From an alchemical point of view, Psyche is lunar, while Eros is solar. Both the Sun and the Moon have a home in darkness in the hidden valley before they emerge into the light.

It is useful to remember that Eros is also associated with the dragon or ancient serpent, a being thought, in alchemy, to have two paradoxical qualities. One of these is the destruction necessary to reduce our reactive habit body to its essential nature; the other is an aspect of our essential creative nature. The dragon combines both these degenerative and generative aspects within itself. In a sense, the dragon is the dissolving aspect of our essence that must be united with our creative aspect. Life is a constant cycling and intertwining of the degenerative and generative dynamics.

Intimacy with the Sacred

In the alchemical process of transforming the old body of habits, the bed is considered a vessel for union of male and female essences and the place where the Elixir, the Philosopher's Stone, the essence of Wisdom and authentic aliveness, is conceived.

It is also said that, during this initial stage in the process of growth, we discover the purpose for our presence on Earth, to which we then dedicate our lives. This is the child we hold in our womb, the seed we want to nourish and cultivate. This is not only the purpose, but the signature, of our soul's role in the cosmos. It is discovered during our initial conscious descent and union with love. How we deal with what follows determines whether our contribution is sacred or mundane, divine or of the ordinary.

The period spent in the hidden palace of Eros represents both the breaking with old familiar patterns of childhood during the emergence into early adulthood and the powerful prison of pleasure that emerges when our relationship is devoured by sexual passion without the deeper bonds having been revealed and cultivated. Psyche feels imprisoned by the darkness and the invisible quality of the forces in her life and grows restless with the limitations placed on what she can know and with whom she can relate. In spite of the sense of impending crisis and potential doom she feels, she uses everything in her power to bring additional relationships into her life.

The unseen voices of the palace of Eros in the hidden valley suggest that the sacred is not embodied at this point in the process. Eros himself remains unseen, a partial embodiment that can be felt and heard, but not viewed for who and what he is.

During our own periods in these hidden palaces, we, in our confusion, try to possess or own Love personally, keeping it to ourselves hidden in our secret inner valleys. We fail to realize that, unless we share that loving energy in the world, life will not perpetuate itself and meaning will become dull and uninspiring. By isolating this initial relationship, we deprive ourselves of connection to the world. Love is a great divine gift that can readily withdraw from our presence.

When Doubts Matter and When They Don't

Enter Psyche's sisters. For the sisters, what matters is not the murder of Psyche's husband, but breaking the taboo against actually seeing directly the divine spouse. They want to cause a rift in the relationship between Eros and Psyche, to reveal the agreements the lovers have made that limit the relationship and imprison Psyche. As the power of doubt, the sisters assert their own power over Psyche, the personal soul as learning being.

While it appears that they want to bring the soul back to the ordinary and reassert the primacy of personal, reactive, familial ties, they in fact force Psyche into the next phases of spiritual development, keeping her from settling for only a periodic and felt sense of the Divine. Further, the sisters represent the kinds of unrelenting doubts that can level inequalities, because they attack anyone and anything. They are even willing to leave the service of their own familial relationships. They are the match that ignites the fuel of Psyche's fears and reactions, which in turn leads to the fire that consumes the pretensions of this initial, but incomplete and unequal, union. The sisters serve their purpose of precipitating the next step on the path, but are not the torch that can light the way or fuel the next stages of growth. They lack the trust and stability needed to accomplish the task of psycho-spiritual development. Instead, they empower her to light the torch. Beyond that, they, as carriers of unrelenting doubt, must not impede the progress of the personal soul in its journey toward sacred embodiment.

The sword is an alchemical symbol of the fire of consciousness that operates in the initial stage of the work of the nigredo, or black night, when the old ways go through their first death in their process of dissolution into their *prima materia*. When Psyche spills hot oil on Eros, the wounding indicates the beginning of the process by which the elements are separated so they can be purified. The sword in the myth can be used to destroy or to discriminate. The light of seeing keeps Psyche from using the sword in a destructive way and sets the stage for her to learn discriminating wisdom and its proper use in her development.[1]

Psyche's true relationship to the sacred begins when she shines light on her unseen lover, Eros. Interrupting the sleep of Eros also interrupts the sleep of the lovers in their not-quite-conscious union. What had been only hinted earlier now becomes evident. Thus this new wakefulness becomes the only proof of the existence of the sacred. It pulls the lovers apart, at the same time that it moves them into the necessary path of conscious sacred work, now inspired by the drive to heal the fracture and rebuild the wholeness of the relationship.

When Psyche pricks herself with the arrow of Eros and falls in love with Love, she activates a capacity in herself that inspires her and keeps her connected through all of the challenges that follow. The personal soul as learning being now has a glimpse of the

Divine and becomes totally dedicated to a more complete relation-ship with the sacred. At the very point where this dedication arises and the bond is affirmed, a loss occurs. The glimpse of Eros must sustain her, for it is fleeting and her lack of skill in handling this new kind of passion leads to a wounding, a split from the sacred that seemed at hand.

In my own experience and that of many of my students, I have witnessed the light that emerges when the real beauty and power of the sacred is revealed for the first time. I have also seen the inevitable attempt to grasp that experience and hold on to it, think-ing that the final realization is near. Many get discouraged and depressed when the peak experience dissolves and cannot be retrieved. Others come to know in the core of their being that they are now committed to a path that will retrain their habits of mind and body into the qualities of Wisdom.

In this experience of connection to divine Love and the subse-quent loss, you grow—through the encounter, the grief, and the sacrifices that characterize the work from then on. The sense of the divine Love becomes internalized by your personal soul, even as that soul has made a powerful and recognizable mark on the energy of Love.

The Waters of Loss and Grief

The tears that Psyche sheds before her initial wedding and after Eros has disappeared into the Heavens represent the dissolution that is necessary for each next stage. Tears are a form of the primal waters and heavenly dew. They are the divine blessings of grief and joy that can clarify vision. While we seem to drown in them, they are the waters of grace that purify our heart and prepare us for liv-ing in the sacred.

After Eros flees, Psyche tries to drown herself in the tears of grief. A real suicide here would represent withdrawal from the path by escaping into numbness and becoming a zombie. This zombie presence pollutes the world. To die in this way violates the basic laws of life and nature. So the river of grief simply dissolves Psyche and deposits her on the other shore. This also represents a purification and dissolution of parts of her old self, pushing her to move on and deal with loss.

In times of loss, you may be torn between going numb and extreme indulgence in intense feelings. The real challenge of developing a sense of the spirit, of a deeper, more profound sense of life, lies in learning how to be and live in the middle of strong feelings and pain without shutting down or being overwhelmed.

Once Psyche has left the world of the familiar and experienced the fire of love and meaning, she can no longer return to the old world in the old way. She could have tried to return to her familial home as an angry victim, seeking the sympathy of others and enlisting them in a hostile campaign against fate. But she does none of that. In fact, she makes no attempt to go back to the home of her childhood. Her revenge on her sisters is more like a purge of parts that are no longer needed in her journey to maturity. In the course of her pursuit of divine Love, she promptly rids the story of pernicious, jealous, and angry doubts, even though they were the forces that awakened her and pushed her on the journey.

For the magnificence of our sacred nature to mature, our personal soul must relinquish its acquired reactive habits. This means the clay vessel must be reduced to dust and the dust rewetted to be reshaped by the challenges of sacred meaning, rather than the prescribed routines of ordinary life.

Eros' Task

As Eros reveals when he flees, his initial love of Psyche happened when he saw her and was stung by one of his own arrows. Now he feels the impact of her and it wounds him, because they are not yet ready to bring their union to fruition. She must learn the sacred ways and build skill and capacity, and he must refine and mature his radiant and connective powers so they can create a new order, a new sacred body.

The deathly wound to Eros hints at possible associations with Osiris, who was fatally wounded and brought back to life by his Mother/Sister/Wife, Isis. Eros goes through his own kind of resurrection through the care of Aphrodite and the guidance of Sobriety, who teaches him virtue and discipline. Discipline derives from the word "disciple," which comes from *discere*, meaning "learning that derives from love and awe." Part of Eros' task requires that he develop discipline. We get the sense that his presence in the home of Aphrodite, where Psyche is being challenged, serves as a support for her successfully accomplishing her tasks. It is possible that the discipline he is learning is also being made available to Psyche in the form of surrogates—ants, reed, eagle, and tower.

Moving on from the Devastation of Loss

A number of dangers arise in the calcination and dissolution phases of the alchemical transformation. Nihilism, an extreme denial of existence, meaning, and value, can seem very attractive as a viewpoint when we indulge in the despair that often arises. We risk becoming overly self-preoccupied. Another troubling reaction to this process takes an opposite course. During dissolution, the melting of personality traits may feel blissful and freeing, making us ripe for seduction into the desire to simply merge with some spaced-out, undifferentiated state of false understanding and sense of oneness. Mind-altering drugs can readily produce this sense of self-dissolution.

Whether our experience is being numbed out or hyped up, drug-dependent states do not last and, in the case of habituation or addiction, actually diminish our capacity for realization and embodiment. One of the important lessons of the myth and of alchemy centers on the dedication necessary for bringing the hidden seeds of wisdom to fruition by incarnating them in our own physical realities and bringing these fruits to our communities.

The paradox of deep wounding is that it can demonstrate both the robustness of your spiritual capacity and your incurable sense of fragility about your own life. Each aspect of your being, your Psyche, and your Eros, must now take on the task of making relationships whole before the eyes of Heaven and Earth. They cannot go back to the secret relationship of the past, nor can they take the old forms into the new light. The light of insight and consciousness has made the situation irreversible.

As in the story, our personal soul moves from a series of ruptures—torn from the familial home, kept from seeing the beloved, betrayed by the sisters, betraying and wounding Eros, abandoned by Eros, unsupported by Demeter and Hera, challenged by Aphrodite, and overcome by deadly sleep—to the rapture of the divine wedding and sacred birth. These ruptures in connection are not a sign of degradation, but of the necessary breaks we must go through and the separations we must experience to grow into our full potential for connection and realization. The rapture of realization and embodiment is seeded in the soil of ruptures that have been fully lived.

One of the points of the myth is that there is a personal legacy being molded from our journey that gives testimony to our life. In a life unlived at the level of the heart and shut off from the world of the sacred, this legacy is a desert, a wasteland of numbness and hidden wounds, of longing and indulgence, of fear and reaction. Our very efforts to make something of these inner landscapes of desolation, so often recreated in the outer world by our misuse, exploitation, and carelessness, begins to reveal a strength of character and vision.

Chapter Eleven

THE QUALITIES OF THE SACRED

We let ourselves be enslaved in order to achieve freedom.

SAMUEL BAK

The process of sorting the grains and seeds is known in alchemy as separation. Separation is the process of discernment of what is of real value and discrimination between the mundane and sacred dimensions of being. We discard what is unnecessary and tap our resources in newly useful ways. A calm consciousness and sustained attention emerges. Finally and most important, we get a glimpse of our essential nature in the calm abiding that arises as we become adept at the process.

Separation occurs in all four tasks assigned by Aphrodite. The first explicitly requires that, from the chaotic jumble that represents her confused mind, Psyche sort the grains and seeds into order. In the second, she must discern the way to approach the divine fire of the rams to gather just the amount of golden fleece required. The third demands that she obtain the water of life as opposed to the water of death. She separates the flow of the sacred from the everyday. She discerns those qualities that may have energy but do not support new life, from those that support the growth and embodiment of sacred Wisdom.

The fourth task begins with another process of separation—between Heaven, Earth, and the Underworld, and between the life and death aspects of the cycles of time. A further distinction (separation) is made between the irreversible journey to the world of the dead through physical death, and the conscious journey that can be taken by an initiate under the guidance of a spiritual system. In the journey to the Underworld, we learn about the need to distinguish between the requirements of the journey and the distracting temptations along the way in the realm of the dead. These various levels of separation bring increasing clarity as we begin to see beyond the surface of appearances and reactions.

The story tells us that, in order to live a sacred life, we must reconstruct ourselves, rebuilding our body of habits (mental, emotional, and physical) piece by piece. Only by patiently sorting each habit of thought and feeling, each a seed for future reaction and experience, can we expect to acquire a power of attention and consciousness of our present condition. This preparation takes time and, in some respects, never stops as part of sacred conscious work. As soon as we become mindful of all that has accumulated in our body of habits, we acquire new habits and the task continues. As soon as we open a space, new experiences and learnings etch their marks on our soul. The key now is to make it all part of our conscious work and use it to mature into profound Wisdom and create sacred beauty.

The Beginning of the Conscious Journey

Psyche begins the process of sorting at the temple of Demeter. This is the beginning of her conscious journey, in contrast to her unconscious wanderings. At this point, she is reminded that this is only a start. In other words, she has made the right steps by being mindful and invoking the sacred dimension of being, but this must not be mistaken as a solution to the problems of life or a quick path to spiritual realization. So she is told to take up the journey again and continue the work.

At the temple of Hera, also known as the "Ox-eyed" (a symbol of spontaneous cognition and intuition of the true nature of being), Psyche is directed by the wisdom of Hera to turn from a path guided by longing to a path on which she confronts her real teacher, Aphrodite, who holds the key teachings and the power that will challenge her into authentic growth. When she hears the call of Hermes, god of Wisdom and bridge between the mundane and the sacred, she finally accepts the challenge of undertaking sacred transformation that is a qualification for the authentic union with divine aliveness, Eros.

Even having made that decision, the story indicates that we will continue to be assaulted by "Old Habit" as we enter this difficult and unknown path. Old reactive habits haunted us in the past, but as we embark on the road of consciousness, they become more obvious and this recognition tears us apart, further breaking down our old identities and attachments.

Creating the Conscious Pause

In the first task, a grain is considered a seed of the metals in the physical world and a particle of thought in the inner world. The seeds that are sorted in the story are the infinite kernels of meaning that make up the rich inner and outer world. Just as our physical body separates nutrients for growth, our head and our heart, representing our body of thoughts and feelings, must sort meanings and values, separating them from each other and ourselves from the demanding world of habits.

In dealing with the enormity of this first task, Psyche becomes very still. Paralysis at a reactive level means going numb. Here, however, the context is the sacred domain, and, at a spiritual level, we can read Psyche's response as representing the kind of pause that allows the natural forces to unfold. Psyche is reduced to her basic nature as Life Force and an open learning being. As a learning being, she is a vessel for the teachings, the sacred experiences, and the emerging fruit of her journey. She is making the transition from simply being a personal soul to growing into a Sacred Soul.

Psyche needs to recreate the process of original creation of the macrocosm in the microcosm. Thus her first actively spiritual task is the sorting of grains and seeds that are in a state of chaos. This allows her to make distinctions and discriminations paralleling what the ancient Eros did with primal Chaos at the beginning of time.

In talking about the soul, we must deal with its paradoxical nature. The chaos of thoughts and feelings that make up the reactive habit body cannot be sorted by imposing order. The process involves creating enough mindful space to include everything. From this space, Psyche can evaluate what is important and what is not. This is done more by the heart than the head, for the heart can be more spacious, not confined by the strictures of thought. From this openness, an order emerges that is beyond conceptual explanation.

The ants represent a nondirected order. There is no leader or foreman that supervises the activities of each ant, yet they are able to work in teams and to build elaborate collectives. The teaming chaos of an ant colony is structured and orderly in ways that defy ordinary explanation.[1]

Psyche makes her way through the tasks on what appears to be ever-shifting ground, as Aphrodite escalates the magnitude of the tasks presented to this aspiring occupant of Heaven. The journey that Psyche takes calls upon her to draw on unknown and unsuspected sources of clarity, strength, and courage. The demands faced by both Psyche and Eros are recognized primarily by those who have entered or are entering the path of deeper meaning and more expanded spiritual aliveness.

The ants in the first task, the reed in the second, and the eagle in the third arise from areas of human nature that are generally unnoticed until we make a conscious journey into the sacred. They represent capacities for clarity and truth that are cultivated through the discipline of conscious spiritual work. Their potential for transformation of our way of being can only be realized when placed in the service of a sacred purpose, divine love as represented by both Aphrodite and Eros.

Even the thought of Eros, who is absent in form but present in Psyche's mind, is the added element that completes the conditions for the emergence of sacred forces. The heart posture of love and the intention to be in relationship with the forces of love set the frame. The relationship orients both Eros and Psyche so that their efforts and trials move in the right direction. Even the mistakes point in the right direction, as when Psyche opens the casket from Persephone.

Air of Insight and Fire of Passionate Wisdom

In the second task, Psyche is guided by the wind passing through a reed. The reed is associated with the capacity to convey secret knowledge or divine Wisdom when the wind whistles through it.[2] Wind, or air, is the movement that brings things together and infuses everything with the life of creation. It is the primordial breath of original creation. It is also the symbol of a consciousness that can bring freshness and new possibilities into being. The spirit, as the Divine taking form, is usually characterized as light, or wind, or both. Embodying movement, the wind was there from the beginning and represents the eternal presence of pure being.

Gaston Bachelard called the element of air "the psychic growth hormone" because of its constant movement and changes that provide the foundation for transformation. Wind, breath, spirit, *chi*, *prana*, *lun*, and *ruach* are all terms for a life-force energy in different traditions and languages. In alchemy, air is considered as invigorating and a bringer of insight. During the second task, the wind, using the instrument of the reed, inspires Psyche and offers her the insights necessary to capture the power of a truly sacred inspiration.

The secret fire of alchemy is the Wisdom energy implicit in inspiration that is represented in the story as the golden fleece, the fire of the ram of the Sun.[3] Psyche only gathers as much as needed. It is easier to contain a measured amount of heat that is meant to nourish our growth than a great quantity that can burn us up. In performing the second task, Psyche is advised to pay attention to the rhythms of the day and to the intensity of the forces at work on the rams. She is called upon to develop patience in obtaining this valuable Wisdom energy.

The secret fire, also represented in the person of Eros, shows up later in the story with the process of fermentation, when Eros comes to Psyche to awaken her from the dead. Alchemically, the subtle or sacred essence is extracted from the gross material of everyday physical existence. *The Emerald Tablet* states that this phase of the process must be done "gently and with great ingenuity." "Gently" suggests that we must proceed with conscious awareness and care. As Dennis Hauck suggests, "ingenuity" means "inspired by genius" or "infused with spirit."

Even as we develop mindfulness and concentration, in this task we are told through the image of the golden rams that we must add the fiery threads of passionate wisdom to bring radiance to the fabric, the skin of our new sacred body. Every thread of this divine wool forms a practice of love for wisdom, life, and creation—a sacred philosophy (*philo*, "love"; *Sophia*, "wisdom") that we wear as a divine garment to remind us of our passionate Wisdom nature.

Water of Transformative Aliveness

The water of Styx is so powerful that it holds all existence, mundane and sacred, in its grip of birth and death.[4] For the spiritual alchemist, working with Styx involves both the possibility of death and the promise of rebirth. The water in the third task, water of life from the point where the river of death transforms to the river of life, is itself a vessel of transformation. This water, which carries the nutrients of wisdom and value from those in the land of the dead to those in the land of the living, enhances the experience of life and intensifies the vibration of aliveness. The radiance of wisdom must be enlivened from the river of life and death that flows continuously, every drop a moment in time and a gateway to eternity. The fluidity of the river keeps us always adaptable and fresh from one moment to the next. This precious, adaptable liquid is extracted and carried by an eagle. The eagle, in alchemy, represents the stage of the white tincture or silver wisdom, a state of motion.

The cup for the third task is an *alembic* (limbeck), an alchemical vessel made of glass or crystal. The crystal goblet also represents the white stage or *albedo* of the alchemical process. This stage is nearly pure and turns experience into the silver of Wisdom, a perfection of the virtues and the development of the subtle energies of Wisdom. This phase is still shy of complete embodiment, but is a foundation for the final stages of embodiment and pure manifestation of divine Wisdom.

With the final stages, we can die to our old forms, our old habit body, and be reborn in a new, sacred way that embodies the marriage of our learning being, our Life Force, our personal soul, to Love, the Sacred. We move into authentic relationship as a member of the community of sacred powers and qualities that go back to the very origin of existence and forward into all futures.

While the acquisition of love, wisdom, and bliss is appealing, minimizing the dangers and the difficulties of the path of the initiate can falsify what is required and trivialize its result. In following the path indicated here, our world is shattered and broken, and our enormous efforts to put it back together again in the old way, as we are inclined to do, face the impossibility of binding the fragments to recreate the old mold. Yet, after being beaten again and again by old habit, we can still make something of those fragments by seeing in a new way, living with the brokenness, and letting a new sense of aliveness and wholeness emerge that provides a new landscape for our experience. This new beauty will always have the hint of destruction somewhere, even if it is only the sense of having gone through great loss, grief, and death on the way to a newly found aliveness and happiness.

Chapter Twelve

DEATH AND REBIRTH

The Creation Mother is always also the Death Mother and vice versa. Because of this dual nature, or double-tasking, the great work before us is to learn to understand what around and about us and what within us must live, and what must die. Our work is to apprehend the timing of both; to allow what must die to die, and what must live to live.

CLARISSA PINKOLA ESTÉS

The insights, clarity, and unleashed energy that flows from the breakdown of old habit structures and the reordering of inner ideas and forces gives us the foundation for taking on the most stubborn belief systems and attitudes that tie us to a limiting, pretentious existence. Our unproductive and enslaving attachments to our material, mental, and emotional habits and identities are the focus of our attention in the early stages of our conscious work. Now, in moving beyond the purifying and clarifying stages, we will work with the most basic issues of life and death, and with the essential aspects of Love and the Soul.

In this story, the steps of fermentation, distillation, and conjunction take place in the performance of the fourth task. Learning about the realm of the dead sets the stage for the deathly sleep that

Psyche has carried from the Underworld. This death removes the final traces of reactive fears, hopes, and habits. Our habit body is now ready to be discarded in favor of a sacred body. This requires the infusion of spiritual energy from divine Love. Only this sacred intense energy can shock us into the next level of conscious realization and embodiment. In our engagement in the fourth task, all of these phenomena are revealed, showing us as initiates how to navigate the dangerous waters of the encounter with death and the uncertain process of rebirth.

When Psyche is given her final task, she knows of only one way to reach the queen of the dead and the world of darkness. For the untrained mind, it seems that we must experience physical death to gain the blessed wisdom hidden within it. Once again, the thought of suicide occurs to Psyche.

In a sense, each thought of suicide contains a death and, from a spiritual point of view, a metamorphosis (*meta*, "beyond"; *morphos*, "death") or transformation. At a reactive psychological level, suicide constitutes an escape from the challenge of living, even as we sense that life itself is at stake. At a symbolic level, each virtual encounter with death can represent the death of a contractive part and a rebirth into a more spiritually connected quality of wisdom. At a spiritual, conscious-work level, such thoughts represent the willingness to put your life as it has been known on the line and to die to your old self, surrendering to the mystical forces of the sacred in bringing forth the fruit of new wisdom.

Guidance in this fourth task comes from a tower. The tower in alchemy is a synonym for the *athanor*, or furnace of wisdom that is an essential tool in the work of attaining profound wisdom. In the story, this tower is part of the palace of Aphrodite, a part of the system constructed to provide a home for divine energy. It encompasses the spiritual exercises of Aphrodite involved in a ritual of approaching death and rebirth. (This also resonates with the mystery systems of Isis and Osiris alluded to in the last parts of *Transformations*, Apuleius' larger work that contains this story.)

The tower instructs Psyche to enter a particular cave that leads to the home of darkness, the Underworld of Tartarus, governed by Hades and Persephone. Tartarus represents the lower world, hell. In alchemy, this world is thought to be composed of the detritus, the sediment and waste, thrown off by the living world. All beings on their journey to a reawakened life must pass through this world, and it is from this residual domain that new life emerges. Hell, in alchemy, is a name for the black or dark aspect of the *prima materia* that existed in primal Darkness. It also represents a stage of the process of dying and leaving behind old forms and habits prior to being reborn into a new life of wisdom.

This journey into the cave is a form of dark retreat—a solitary journey done in darkness designed to bring forth the essential qualities of authentic presence, the energies of aliveness, silence and listening, and the sacred wisdom of having lived beyond the ordinary world. In the dark, all of our physical, mental, and emotional habitual patterns become evident. We sense both the flows and fields of energy in our body, and they often take visible form in the external environment of the dark. In the dark, we learn to be more open and inclusive, yet precise, in relation to our actions. We also realize that everything that arises comes from that space of darkness, exists within its nature, and dissolves into that space.[1]

Many of the prophets of ancient Israel and the oracles of ancient Greece retreated to caves or dark places to receive Divine Wisdom. For these prophets and oracles, the task involved giving voice to what is beyond the ordinary and becoming a spokesperson for the Divine. Followers of the philosophical and mystical practices at the time of Apuleius were familiar, not only with the works of Plato, but also with the teachings of Pythagoras and Parmenides. Peter Kingsley argues that the practices of the mystical teachings of Pythagoras involved, among their various exercises, the use of "incubation in darkness."[2] The world of night and darkness for Parmenides is the unknown home of wisdom, in the land that is called "ignorance" in ordinary life, because people who run from death ignore the very place that is the source of wisdom.

For the Greeks, the home of Apollo is the Underworld of darkness, that place whence the Sun arises and returns every day. The source of the light of wisdom has its home in darkness. In the time of the ancient Greeks, many of the priests who worked in the temples of Apollo, considered a god of incubation along with Dionysus, spent days in the caves beneath the temples in total darkness, surrendering to another level of awareness and emerging from this descent with new wisdom and teachings for the world.

The descent into darkness and the dying that constitute the initial phase of fermentation are often called the "dark night of the soul." This phase of fermentation is also called by alchemists putrefaction. In fermentation, we are on fire with inspiration and dedication, and flooded with profoundly meaningful visions and insights totally beyond our normal personal reality. In the story, Psyche is advised to abstain from dining with Persephone during her fermentation in the Underworld. In part, this proscription cautions us from indulging in the hellish comforts of blame and victimhood. For alchemists, this represents the "fermentation fast" that prepares us for the break with worldly routines and stimuli, and the switch to being nourished by sacred energies and divine qualities.

The journey to the world of darkness is seen by the Wisdom practitioners of ancient Greece and alchemists of later ages as engaging the fire of the Underworld that has the power to purify and transform us. Every phase of the cycles of light and dark must be made part of the process of growth. There are no short cuts. To find the wisdom that lies beyond the surface of experience means facing utter darkness and the teachings of death. This is the journey that Psyche takes in this task.

Into the Dark

Darkness, in its mundane usage, refers to ignorance as the absence of the light of truth. As mentioned earlier, this can also mean the domain that is ignored in everyday life, namely the sacred. Darkness in its sacred aspect is the source—the primal, formless nature of all being, the Absolute, the potential, the unknowable, the unmanifest. It is the Mystery of all mysteries.[3]

In this encounter with death and in the journey through the world of the dark, the story indicates that we must not get distracted by the requests of others, by the possibilities of intervening in fate, or by the treasures we may find there. The river Styx, in this world, is the dividing line between the mundane and the sacred, between being stuck in the suffering of reactive identities that persist even beyond physical life and being transported across this river of grief to the sacred palace of wisdom.

Charon, another son of Erebus, who is also a father to the primal Eros, symbolizes the desire and mental grasping nature that propels us through the lower consciousness of the world of ignorance and, when paid a price in the coinage of sacrificed desire, will carry us on his ferry to and from our meeting with death so we can bring the wisdom of this primal world to life.

Cerberus, the three-headed dog, guardian of the palace of Hades, symbolizes the threefold aspects of consciousness—Will (Relationship), Wisdom (Space), and Activity (Energy)—made manifest on the lower planes of being.

Persephone, the Queen of the Underworld, is a mentor who knows about death and the cycle of rebirth, knows about beauty and its place in all worlds—the Underworld, Earth, and Heaven—and knows about living in both the world of the dead and the living (she emerges every spring.)

Relating to death with deep understanding is essential for transformation at many levels. Without death, meaning is in danger of becoming trivial. Part of the beauty of death is the way it highlights the radiance of life. With death as a presence, significance intensifies and worth is placed in perspective. Death is paradoxically both a creator of a hierarchy of worth and a leveler of all beings because there is no being, no thing, no manifestation that escapes its grasp.

Bringing the Wisdom of the Dark into the Light

As we emerge from the palace of Hades and Persephone, we are engaged in a process of distilling the essence of the wisdom and energy that will support living in all the worlds. These new inspirations, visions, and life energies are further refined in the process of distillation. Residues of our old habit body are left behind as we are called by the Heavens to realize our most worthy nature and cultivate our most valuable wisdom qualities. In our work of distillation, we extract the motile spirit from the material of our lives. We capture the essential energy from reaction and leave the shell of old habits behind. This return to Earth with what has been distilled in the work in Heaven and in Hell can now serve to sanctify the ordinary world of our everyday life.

Psyche returns from the world of the dead with the invisible beauty of the teachings from the queen of death in a box, or casket, which is considered an alchemical vessel for containing this wisdom. Yet at this point, she is still not quite ready for final realization and embodiment. She needs to be overwhelmed in order to move through this shock point into the sacred life that can only be achieved through a kind of rebirth. The rebirth must include, not only the personal soul, but also sacred Love. Our learning being must disintegrate and be reintegrated by Love before becoming the body of wisdom that makes it possible for us to enter the company of the wise.

Rising from the dead to another dimension of being and aliveness is called "transformation" and "quickening." In the story, as in alchemy, this transformational aspect of fermentation involves being infused by spirit (Eros) and rising, much as yeast bread rises. This process, in its maturing aspect, is likened to the creation of alcohol, particularly wine.

Psyche's sleep of death is the long-delayed death spoken of by the oracle at the beginning of the story. This is Psyche's more complete and final death as transformation into a new life. Her journey took her from a lovely, innocent, frightened, and perhaps self-preoccupied child, to the challenges of life's complexities and paradoxes, to the painful but eventually blissful realization of her potential as the creator of new life, new wisdom, and loving connection.

The lessons and beauty that are brought back in the casket are more than the personal soul can handle without the full presence of Divine Love. At this point, Eros is healed and resurrected from his own kind of death. Now, inspired by a more mature love of his own, he seeks a reunion with the Life Force, the Soul. Love, as compassion, can gather all the overwhelming qualities of the wisdom and beauty of death and life.

The divine energy and consciousness of Love can gather the deathly residues, containing them and injecting new meaning and heart postures into us. We are revived in a new way following this reunion with the Divine Spirit. Our authentic way of being, with its greater consciousness, is now ready to move more fully into the sacred. We approach the final stage of initiation of our soul, our now-sacred learning being, into the world of clarity beyond the illusions of the surface layer of ordinary life. The type of distillation that occurs in the story during this death and rebirth phase is often called sublimation, the transformation of something solid into a gaseous state or, in this case, the transformation of the soul and love from rigid forms into fresh, open, and sublime qualities of the spiritual.

In this final phase of distillation, Eros and Psyche, having been briefly conjoined, once again separate as part of the final refinement of the forces of Life and Love, in preparation for their final union. This process, like all the others, may take some time to bring about. We must intensify our efforts at this point to create the conditions for the embodiment of peace, radiance, love, and wisdom as we grow into becoming a more complete vehicle for Divine Wisdom and presence in the world.

Chapter Thirteen

REALIZATION AND
EMBODIMENT

We then, who are this new soul, know,
Of what we are composed and made...

So must true lovers' souls descend
T'affections, and to faculties . . .
To our bodies turn we then, that so
Weak men on love revealed may look;
Love's mysteries in souls do grow,
But yet the body is his book.

JOHN DONNE, "THE EXTASIE"

In alchemy the process for achieving the conscious state of clarity and Wisdom is often divided into three broad stages that are called *magistries.* The first represents gaining control of our body and finding complete relaxation and peace. The second involves control of our mind by inspiration and discipline. In the third, the union of body and mind, of soul and spirit, frees us from the limitations of habit, environment, and even inherited tendencies. In this third stage, we manifest our authentic presence and express the bliss of profound clarity and love.

The Chemical Wedding

Psyche, now the daughter of Aphrodite and a mature Sacred Soul, ascends for her union with the son of Aphrodite, who is a disciplined and refined Love. They have both passed through the challenging tests of the Divine Mother. The third union brings together the distilled essence of Eros and the fermented Psyche in a divine coagulation that becomes an abiding consciousness and spiritual presence clarifying all experience and generating beneficial qualities in the world.

The final marriage, called in alchemy the "chemical wedding," is presided over in Heaven by Zeus, who represents, not only the supreme Wisdom, but also the force that can integrate all the qualities and energies of sacred and ordinary life.[1] Aphrodite dances at this wedding to show her approval of and joy in this union of her son, who has matured as a force of Love, and her daughter, whom she has mentored through all the stages and challenges the personal soul must encounter in order to realize its divine essence. At this time, each main character is revealed in its true identity as realized potential: Eros as binding refined Love, Psyche as a Divine Beauty crafted through grief and challenge, and Aphrodite as mentor and guide.

We can imagine that what concerned Aphrodite in the beginning, among the many issues of pretension, revolved around a question of conversation. She wanted her son to marry someone of her level, someone with whom she could talk for long hours about the state of the Heavens and the Earth, and someone who, when her belly was ready, would give issue to a being that could boast of irreproachable ancestry.

The successive unions of Eros and Psyche create new constellations of beliefs and forces that are less tied to material convention and increasingly aligned with the Heavens and Sacred Wisdom. In the final union of Heaven, the soul of the body is made spiritual and the spiritual is embodied. The resulting consciousness and rapture then exists in all dimensions of being.

The Elixir of Eternal Life and the Stone of Embodiment

The symbols that alchemists use for the final state include precious stones, gold, a child, salt, an Elixir (the nectar of the gods and ambrosia of immortality). The Elixir and the Philosopher's Stone are considered the same essence, the Elixir being the liquid form, and the Stone being solid or powder.

The Elixir is the principle of life itself that nourishes the Life Force and blesses existence and meaning with vitality and the spirit of life. Nectar, as the Elixir, is divine consciousness and sacred energy. Honey is a term for the Elixir, because it is sweet and golden in color. Honey is also another reference to the bee that is associated with Eros. Just as the Elixir is the wisdom principle of vitality, the Philosopher's Stone or diamond is the wisdom principle of clarity. This clarity is more than insight; it is the very open, clear light of awareness that is the foundation of all existence.

Life is transformed from an habitually reactive and numb existence to the experience of aliveness, awakened and engaged in the presence of the world. This aliveness dwells in each moment and each moment constitutes an eternity, beyond time and space. Aliveness is the eternal presence manifesting in your experience.

In alchemical literature, the infant Philosopher's Stone is sometimes personified as a female child who represents Wisdom and the rapture of the wise way of being. The Stone is a transformative jewel that can turn base metals into pure gold, reactive experience into Wisdom, and you, as an earthly being, into the embodiment of sacred Wisdom and divine Love. The Stone is thought of in paradoxical and enigmatic ways. Democritus, around 350 B.C.E., supposedly said that "it is a stone and not a stone."[2]

The Philosopher's Stone represents sacred Wisdom, authentic aliveness, and beneficial presence in the service of the world. This is the essence of profound wisdom. The final clear, indestructible diamond state is made of the same material as the soft, black coal of our beginning state of confused and reactive consciousness. Only now it has been transformed by the successful application of conscious work to the pressures of life—life made completely aware and energized and in loving relationship to the world.

The marriage of Eros and Psyche brings forth a new quality into reality, a daughter who incorporates attributes of her parents. Rapture includes the passion of Love and the fullness of the Life Force, the fire of Spirit and the expanding container of the Soul. This daughter is born beyond linear time in the eternal. She tears the fabric of ordinary time and space with her cry—the vibration of the sublime holy.

This union moves the relationship from pleasure to rapture and bliss, *voluptas* (life filled with delight). *Voluptas*, the Latin word used by Apuleius in his story, is not simply pleasure, for that had been known before, if only in its mundane sense. Rather it is a divine pleasure that is realized as a way of being, a rapture from which all life can be filled with the joy of relationship. In addition, this rapture also results in an intensity of being. The final state of rapture, bliss, and divine pleasure cannot be described by conceptual language. This delicious, undifferentiated, fully vibrant, ecstatic, and open state involves our entire being, the whole of our body-mind, which is no longer ours, but a manifestation of all being. We are completely enthusiastic, in the original meaning from the Greek *enthous* (to be possessed by the gods).

In searching for the appropriate word for this state, I have chosen rapture and yet I mean that word to also include ecstasy and bliss. Rapture is defined as a state of being transported by a lofty emotion, ecstasy. It is an expression of ecstatic feeling. Rapture transports us from one place to another, particularly

Heaven. To be "rapt" is to be deeply moved, delighted, and absorbed.

The word "ecstasy," deriving from *ek* (out, outside of) and *histani*(to place), also conveys the sense of being carried away, transported beyond our usual place and being beside ourselves with joy. Martín Prechtel calls this "a trance of delight or madness that arrests the whole mind."[3] Ecstasy is the state of intense delight in which we are beyond control, beyond the usual, and thus beyond stasis. The word "bliss" refers to extreme happiness and the spiritual joy of being at home in the sacred. Bliss is also equated with ecstasy and rapture.

The mystical literature identifies two aspects of rapture (ecstasy, bliss): total absorption in pure emptiness or openness, and the fullness of presence experienced when we are unified with the totality of manifestation. The rapture of aliveness engenders a quality of presence in the world that radiates a loving field. This ecstasy is itself transformative, for the world is vividly perceived, joyously met, and gratefully embraced. Alchemical rapture results from the process of turning the lead of our everyday experience into the gold of Wisdom energy. Transformation of our mental/physical activity into conscious experience is the bliss of consciousness, the divine pleasure, the pleasure that serves the sacred rather than the ordinary. We must go through tasks and development to give birth to rapture rather than simple pleasure. We must mature beyond our reactions and grow into a conscious being that uses everything in the service of life and a greater purpose.

Rapture is not a reward, but the natural condition of embodiment that comes from navigating the sacred passage through the straits of life, surrounded by the beautiful cliffs of death and grief, with consciousness, stamina, discipline, and an open heart. The embodiment of rapture radiates Aliveness and Love from the inside out, making our heart a source of light for all the world.

The issue of the union of Eros and Psyche is a new body, a bliss body. In tantric Buddhism, this is call *sambhogakaya*. This body is filled with the jewels of conscious meaning and lived experience. The bliss found here is the bliss of aliveness experienced even in painful situations. It connects pain to the sacred, allowing us to transcend the mundane by including an element of divine consciousness in our experience.

The longing of the Life Force as personal soul can only be realized as mature love and relationship if our reactive habit body is torn apart and retrained by the tasks of the goddess. From this new soul, married to the power of refined Love, issues a never-before-experienced rapture, an ecstasy that remains eternally fresh and delicious in every alive, authentic moment, always in service to the world and to the happiness, growth, and true freedom of all beings.

This child of the marriage of Eros and Psyche, Rapture, also represents the bliss of finding and living your own unique manifestation of the Divine, illuminating the world with the particular radiance that only you can bring, and giving to the sacred the blessings that only you can offer.

Chapter Fourteen

MAKING THE MYTH YOUR OWN

*Initiation essentially aims to go beyond the possibilities of
the individual human state to make possible the transition
to higher states and finally to lead the individual
beyond any limitations whatsoever.*

René Guénon in *Glimpses of Initiation*

M any people go through the motions of living, loving,
and enjoying life. Few experience the passionate fullness that is possible beyond daily routines, passive
addictive entertainment, and a nagging sense of dissatisfaction with
the reactive, habitual experience of life. Few live with the moment-
to-moment inspiration of Eros. Few have allowed the depth of grief
to carve their souls with the chisel of loss. Few have allowed the fire
of Love to inflame the heart with sacred significance, forging an
unbreakable bond with all life and with the Divine. Your job, your
home, your property, your investments, your busy-ness, all of
which are meant to give you freedom from fear and insecurity,
actually enslave you through their demands on your time, energy,
and attention. It often takes a profound wound to wake us up and
begin the process of discovery of true freedom.

When we are cut off from the presence of Eros, of living love and connection, we experience an exile from our home in the sacred and in the world. Our longing for belonging may drive us to seek many substitutes for the sacred connection that is in our nature, but obscured by our fears, hopes, and needs.

One purpose of this book has been to revitalize the story of Eros and Psyche and make its sacred dimensions come alive again within you. Our sacred traditions hold treasures beyond value hidden in ancient myths, esoteric teachings, mystic visions, and secret practices that have been passed down from generation to generation.

The myth of Eros and Psyche gives us, as the audience, the lofty position of witness to the drama, much as the gods witness the activities of humans. Through the story, we travel on the Earth, find a home in the hidden valley and then in the Heavens, get to know the heights and the depths of experience, and expose ourselves to the dynamic transformations that are the possibilities of the spiritual. Thus we make ourselves godlike in order to begin to realize and access the qualities of the Divine.

The story travels a path of initiation that takes us from ordinary reactive habits, through fear, inspiration, loss, grief, longing, the assaults of old habits, the discipline of virtue and sobriety, the challenges and tasks of growth, the confrontation with death, the support of the Divine, the ingesting of the nectar of wisdom, to the place of authentic eternal alchemical marriage in the sacred community that brings rapture into the world from a place beyond time and space. On the path, we, as practitioners of conscious work, realize that the stages of the process are a retraining of our soul into the cultivation of the dimensions of being that already exist, and have always existed. We do not create the sacred, rather we move our attention there and allow it to inform our perceptions, ways of thinking and feeling, and actions.

You are called upon to rebuild on the ruins of the old, guided not by hope or despair, but by wonder and Wisdom. In the myth, hope is important as a motivation, but dangerous as a guide (as when Psyche opens the casket from Persephone hoping for divine beauty). Despair may open you up if you do not become too self-preoccupied, but it always creates confusion concerning the appropriate path to take.

As an initiate internalizing the story, you have all of the characters and qualities within yourself. You are a microcosm of the macrocosm, the entire universe. The same forces that shape all existence are present in you. This is the basis of spiritual alchemy and the Doctrine of Correspondences. No matter what your life situations are or how reactively conditioned you have become, you have all the elements within you to free yourself and create benefit in the world.

To do this great work of transformation, you must use your active soul in a sturdy spiritual body. Your active soul is consciously growing and fresh. A well-developed spiritual body is manifest in sacred postures of the heart, such as compassion, clarity, and generosity. Your active soul dedicates itself to cultivating your spiritual body.

The Psyche part of you can feed on anything, from the gold of special moments to the lead of disappointment, from the edge of fear to the edge of love, from the agitation of doubt to the excitement of inspiration. Your soul is always internalizing experience in order to nourish the fetus of the future. It will scavenge through the detritus of the material realm or feast on the delights of the sacred. Your job is to point it in the right direction and nourish it with authenticity and sacred connection.

Psyche, as the "new Aphrodite," can only play at such a role in the beginning, but eventually grows into it as the particular embodiment in form of a universal Wisdom energy. Your personal soul as learning being must cultivate the creative energies of the great goddess of creation in order to make them manifest in yourself. What makes this "new" is the fact that you must give this your own unique expression, even as you follow a universal path.

155

The Eros part of you inclines toward passion and the infusion of the fire of caring and importance into activity. This divine spirit is always striving, always making things significant. It is concerned with the eternal moment and the intensity of the present experience. It is less tied to linear time and the creation of the future, since its source is in sacred time, which is beyond linearity. It concentrates more on the quality of experience than on accumulating experiences. It is not trying to feed anything beyond satisfying the present moment. It is constantly creating and infusing things with the fire of its aliveness, but is not as tied to the material world and human existence.

Just as you ascend, along with Psyche and Eros, to become residents of the sublime realms of existence, so the alchemists aspired to a permanent state of higher consciousness they called the Philosopher's Stone and the Elixir of Life. In the story, you are taken beyond the powers of Aphrodite. The goal is not to become Aphrodite, but to learn from her and understand her wisdom, and then to outgrow and transcend even her influence. This is represented by the ascension to an even higher Heaven and by the birth of a new eternal power. In this way Heaven, what has always been Divine, is changed and transcended in the creation of a new Reality, an even richer Divine Presence.

Surrender in Conscious Work

Working with these teachings requires two forms of surrender or opening. The first involves going into or dissolving outward in Essence. In this experience, a seed becomes the entire universe. Nothing is too much for the opening of this transcendence. It is as if the cells of your body and the particles of your being release their grip on each other. Your form disintegrates, flying outward into the vastness of pure openness. You no longer exist in a particular way. All being, all forms, become your home. You are hosting itself, beyond your hosting and being hosted.

The second is a matter of taking in or hosting the Divine, realizing the Divine in life as Presence. Here hosting and being hosted sing a vital melody of presence. This hosting presence can include everything and give it form. You live with clarity and beauty, dedicated to cultivating and manifesting benefit in the world. You consciously participate in the details, the flows, and the challenges of everyday life. You walk and converse with friends, sensing the wind, and feeling aliveness and joy. The divine shows up through you and through everything. God is manifest.

The fruits of the story's journey are transformation, ecstasy, union, wholeness, divinity, discipline, meaning, belonging, legacy, and maturity. You personally engage life without making the stuff of experience a part of your personality, your personal identity. You do not craft a personal "what" with which you identify. Rather you create an internal atmosphere of ecstasy and an external environment of beneficial presence and beauty.

When you have completed the path, creativity springs from your being. You do not feel creative; you are creative. The creativity springs from your open, natural awareness. You are not self-conscious, but uniquely yourself, without having to inflate yourself with unique qualities. You are part of humanity and the sacred in a unique way, without feeling different from others.

In your inner chemical marriage, you now embody the alchemy of becoming, in that you perceive the act of creation occurring constantly and can see the signature of the Divine in everything. You live in the truth of authentic presence, abiding in Essence, engaged in constant becoming and creation, with the sacred quality of Love, manifesting and sharing Wisdom in the world.

In some versions of the ox-herding drawings of Zen Buddhism, the last in the series shows the herder walking an ordinary country lane, in ordinary clothes, with no distinguishing marks on him. Yet the joy and radiance of his presence causes all the trees to burst into bloom as he passes.

The Sacred Challenge of Life

The myth of Eros and Psyche, in its timelessness, suggests that you live in the midst of a constant flood of disintegration that destroys your certitude. It calls upon you to seize the moment—seize this gift of aliveness before it is too late. It does not say that there are answers to the existential questions of life, that life means this or that. Rather it suggests directions of effort, processes that expand your heart to both embrace what is and to direct your energies always toward improving and changing the conditions of the world by contributing something of beauty and love to it.

Notice that the story does not say that your life problems will be solved or your given time on Earth made easier. It teaches rather that you must greet all of life's cycles with a new heart posture and with sacred confidence. To act with confidence means to behave with fidelity to your own nature, trusting your sacred design. In this way, you give the gift of your authentic presence and deepest self to others and to the sacred dimensions, enlivening the world with beauty and meaning.

The truth of these teachings can only be validated through experience, and experience can only come from enduring practice and continued spiritual growth. You must be willing to go through the painful steps of burning off your pretenses, limiting beliefs, reactive fears and longings. You must follow that with a dissolution of your compulsive and obsessive patterns of thinking, feeling, and behaving.

At the same time, you will begin to perceive the multiple dimensions of being and cultivate the qualities of the sacred. By joining your consciousness with sacred awareness, you host all the various energies that you find within. This inclusion leads to a new harmony. From here, you can cultivate the Wisdom qualities that are a unique expression of your fundamental Wisdom nature.

Continuing the Life of the Story

This story, like so many, is meant to be retold regularly—not simply because additional hidden meanings may become evident, but because it reminds us that the process embedded in the story relates, not only to our overall psycho-spiritual development, but also to the cycles that regularly occur in life. This is work that is never really completed.

The sages say the cycle of this story happens over and over, every day, every season, every year, every lifetime. The rotation of the sky, the cycle of the seasons suggested by the descent and ascent, reminds us that the process will go on happening forever.

We each discover our own lessons in the story, for the possible meanings are innumerable. I have been reading, listening to, and retelling this myth for forty years and, each time, it touches my heart in a new way. Each time, it becomes a new story. So the same story must be repeated with variations so that, through each telling, we may discover a new Ocean, a new Earth, and a new Heaven of meanings, and be reborn into the wondrous world of the sacred.

SYMBOLS AND MYTHICAL AND ALCHEMICAL MEANINGS

Name/Symbol:

Aphrodite (Roman: Venus; Egyptian: Isis; Sumerian: Inanna; Babylonian: Ishtar; Semitic: Asherah)

Mythical Meanings:

A Great Mother Goddess, goddess of love, marriage, sexuality, and childbirth. Associated with the ocean. Primal goddess of creation in some myths.

Alchemical Meanings:

Presides over the sexual union of the male and female seeds of metals/life at the chemical wedding. A force that makes the alchemical union possible.

Name/Symbol:

Eagle

Mythical Meanings:

Soul bird associated with fire, the sun, and lightning; master of vision, the hunt, and the magic of controlling fire; a carrier of wisdom; associated with Zeus.

Alchemical Meanings:

Philosophic mercury that has been sublimated, the white tincture, symbol of a volatile stage of transformation. Associated with air and fire in the alchemical process. Also a symbol for the initiate who has spiritualized the instinctual urges and can use them in conscious work.

Name/Symbol:

Eros (Roman: Cupid)

Mythical Meanings:

Primal god of creation, love, and connection. Offspring of Night and Darkness. Parent of the gods. In this story: god of love/desire, son of Aphrodite. Associated with fire, bees, and dragons.

Alchemical Meanings:

Associated with secret fire, burning water, love essence released by the Elixir of Life or the Philosopher's Stone, bees, honey, dragons.

Name/Symbol:

Golden Fleece

Mythical Meanings:

Heavenly treasure; indwelling fruit of the spirit; form of hidden profound wisdom; the radiance of the rising sun; associated with Zeus.

Alchemical Meanings:

Gold of wisdom that is sought in alchemical work. The "golden fleece" is the name given to the parchment on which the secrets of alchemy are written.

Name/Symbol:

Grains/Seeds

Mythical Meanings:

Latent potentialities; fertility, growth; the Mystic Center.

Alchemical Meanings:

The essence or life spark of metals or the materials from which gold can be generated in the alchemical process. The matter for making the Stone that can reproduce itself.

Name/Symbol:

Hephaestus (Roman: Vulcan)

Mythical Meanings:

Goldsmith to the gods; smith of the heavens; fire god; symbol of the creative mind; husband of Aphrodite and father of Eros in the story; lame.

Alchemical Meanings:

An archetypal alchemist and sometimes considered a symbolic founder of alchemy. Associated with the secret fire of the Work and sometimes one of the facilitators of the birth of the Philosopher's Stone.

Name/Symbol:

Hermes (Roman: Mercury; Egyptian: Thoth)

Mythical Meanings:

God of occult wisdom, communication, medicine, magic, letters, Logos, and learning. Transports souls and has great power over rebirth and reincarnation. Unites both masculine and feminine. God of crossroads.

Alchemical Meanings:

A central symbol of alchemy itself, representing the universal agent of transmutation. It is the alchemist's magical arcanum, the transformative substance without which the entire alchemical process could not happen. Carries the divine love essence which kills falsehood and illusion and allows truth to arise. Participates in both the world of light and of the dark.

Name/Symbol:

Marriage

Mythical Meanings:

Union of Life Force and Wisdom, Life Force and Love, head and heart, lower and higher; death as extinction of sense of separateness or transition from one state to another.

Alchemical Meanings:

Critical operation in the creation of the Philosopher's Stone, also called the "chemical wedding." State where all forces are reconciled and work together in the creation of the gold of eternal wisdom. Union of creative power with wisdom to produce pure love.

Name/Symbol:

Persephone (Roman: Proserpine)

Mythical Meanings:

Queen of the Underworld, goddess of the dead; holds the keys to Heaven and Hell (Elysium and Tartarus); destroyer; daughter of Demeter; symbol of death and rebirth/withdrawal from the world and re-emergence.

Alchemical Meanings:

Holder of the keys to the dissolution, *nigredo*, before one can be reborn in a new form. Associated with one of the death stages of the alchemical process; darkness.

Name/Symbol:

Psyche (Roman: Anima, Animus)

Mythical Meanings:

Life Force; animating quality of life; aliveness; capacity for organic growth, reproduction, perception, thought, independent motion, soul. Capacity for learning. Born of heaven's dew uniting with earth.

Alchemical Meanings:

The volatile vapor released when matter is dissolved in the making of the Philosopher's Stone. It first unites with the spirit in the alchemical wedding (called the "chemical wedding"). Then it is reunited with the material body from which the Stone is born.

Name/Symbol:

Tower

Mythical Meanings:

System of work; rising above common life.

Alchemical Meanings:

Athanor, or philosophical furnace; purifies prior to ascent; transformation and evolution.

Name/Symbol:

Zeus (Roman: Jupiter)

Mythical Meanings:

King of the Heavens; king of the gods; Supreme Wisdom/definer of the order; father figure of the gods and humans; presides over heaven and earth; brother of Poseidon who governs the Ocean and of Hades who governs the Underworld. Sometimes considered a father of Aphrodite and a stepfather of Eros. A face of the Primal Eros of Creation. In later mythology, the son of Cronus (Time) and Rhea (Space).

Alchemical Meanings:

Higher self, carrier of the mystic seed of transcendental life given by Cronus. Philosophical sublimation and the distillation of philosophic gold.

NOTES

Chapter 1

1. My interpretation here is based on passages, images, and text from Aristophanes, Homer, and the Greek myths as presented by Robert Graves. For Aristophanes, see Gilbert Murray, J. H. Frere, and D. K. Sandford, trans., *Ten Greek Plays* (New York: Oxford University Press, 1929); for Homer, see *The Iliad*, Samuel Butler, trans. (Roslyn, NY: Walter J. Black, 1942). Graves gives the following description: "The Orphics say that black-winged Night, a goddess of whom even Zeus stands in awe, was courted by the Wind and laid a silver egg in the womb of Darkness; and that Eros, whom some call Phanes, was hatched from this egg and set the Universe in motion. Eros was double-sexed and golden-winged and, having four heads, sometimes roared like a bull or a lion, sometimes hissed like a serpent or bleated like a ram. Night, who names him Ericepaius and Protogenus Phaëthon, lived in a cave with him, displaying herself in triad: Night, Order, and Justice . . . Phanes created earth, sky, sun and moon, but the triple-goddess ruled the universe, until her scepter passed to Uranus." Robert Graves, *The Greek Myths, Volume One* (New York: George Braziller, 1959), p. 30.

Chapter 2

1. This retelling and translation is based on a number of other translations, as well as my own reading of the Latin. See Erich Neumann, *Amor and Psyche,* Ralph Mannheim, trans. (Princeton, NJ: Princeton University Press, 1965); H. E. Butler, *The Metamorphoses or Golden Ass of Apuleius of Madaura* (Oxford: Clarendon Press, 1910); William Adlington, ed. and trans. in 1566 and revised by S. Gaselee in 1915, *The Golden Ass of Apuleius* (Cambridge: Harvard University Press, 1915); Robert Graves, *The Golden Ass of Apuleius* (New York: Farrar, Straus and Young, 1951); J. Arthur Hanson, *Metamorphoses* (Cambridge: Harvard University Press, 1989); E. J. Kenney, *Cupid and Psyche* (Cambridge, UK: Cambridge University Press, 1990); E. J. Kenney, *The Golden Ass or Metamorphoses* (London: Penguin Classics, 1998).

2. I have used the Greek names to emphasize the story's ancient mythical themes and refer more to the Eleusinian mysteries and the Greco-Egyptian roots of the story in the cult of Isis, who was associated with Aphrodite. In my view, Aphrodite rather than Venus represents the Great Mother Goddess and Eros conveys more of the sense of the mighty primordial god than Cupid, often depicted as simply a mischievous little cherub. For the Greco-Roman-Egyptian reader of Apuleius' day, the words, names, and images carried a history and symbolism that was still alive in their imaginations and sensibilities. Yet they also served to indicate the Greek names hidden beneath the surface, for Apuleius explicitly calls the entire novel a Greek tale. He knew that the unspoken Greek names conveyed a much greater sense of the primordial qualities and energies and that each reference brought an entire history of meaning and connection to those associated with Hellenistic Egypt and the mystery schools that were thriving in North Africa during this time.

Chapter 3

1. Marie-Louise von Franz thinks that "Apuleius . . . had an African unconscious and a Roman consciousness." See *The Golden Ass of Apuleius* (Boston: Shambhala, 1992), p. 11.

2. Graves, *The Golden Ass of Apuleius*, pp. 238–239.

3. For a review of the psychological literature on this myth, particularly the Freudian and Jungian interpretations, see James Gollnick, *Love and the Soul: Psychological Interpretations of the Eros and Psyche Myth* (Waterloo, Ontario: Wilfrid Laurier University Press, 1992).

4. Von Franz believes that "Apuleius intentionally slipped in many symbolic ideas, but that others flowed unconsciously from his pen. Where Apuleius consciously placed certain symbolic motifs in his story, one could be justified in treating them allegorically, in the Platonic sense of the term: as a profound philosophical significance hidden beneath the symbolic image." *The Golden Ass of Apuleius*, p. 3.

5. Paula James, *Unity in diversity : a study of Apuleius' "Metamorphoses": with particular reference to the narrator's art of transformation and the metamorphosis motif in the Tale of Cupid and Psyche* (Hildesheim, Germany: Olms-Weidmann,1987). See also Kenney, *Cupid and Psyche and The Golden Ass or Metamorphoses*; Gollnick, *Love and the Soul*.

Chapter 4

1. See Paula James, *Unity in diversity : a study of Apuleius' "Metamorphoses": with particular reference to the narrator's art of transformation and the metamorphosis motif in the Tale of Cupid and Psyche* (Hildesheim, Germany: Olms-Weidmann, 1987); James Gollnick, *Love and the Soul: Psychological Interpretations of the Eros and Psyche Myth* (Waterloo, Ontario: Wilfrid Laurier University Press, 1992); E. J. Kenney, ed., *Cupid and Psyche* (Cambridge, UK: Cambridge University Press, 1990) and *The Golden Ass or Metamorphoses* (London: Penguin Classics, 1998).

2. Von Franz puts this another way: "Psychological healing always entails a widening of the personality. It brings more life and more aspects of the personality into activity. One can say that the greater part of neurotic disturbances is due to the fact the ego has its shutters too closed against those realities of life which want to enter. Therefore, healing coincides with a widening of consciousness. To the human being this means an access to religious experience, a discovery of the deeper meaning of life and of healing emotions… It also means pulling down a brilliant omnipotent god into the miserable narrowness of human existence." *The Golden Ass of Apuleius* (Boston: Shambhala, 1992), p. 87.

Chapter 5

1. See Robert Graves, *The Greek Myths, Volume 1* (New York: George Braziller, 1959); G. A. Gaskell, *Dictionary of Scripture and Myth* (New York: Dorset Press, 1988); and Marie-Louise von Franz, *The Golden Ass of Apuleius* (Boston: Shambhala, 1992). As von Franz points out, "Certainly in the time of Apuleius, Eros was worshipped as a world-creating principle par excellence; he also played a role in the Mithraic mysteries, where he appears as partner and redeemer of the goddess Psyche," p. 86.

2. Von Franz in *The Golden Ass of Apuleius*, suggests "Eros forces us to become conscious through this (love) tie. Love makes us dare everything and leads us thus to ourselves." p. 83. According to von Franz: "The Greeks identified Eros with Osiris; indeed, for the Egyptians, Osiris taught men and women genuine mutual love," p. 137.

3. According to von Franz, "Psyche personifies . . . some *personal* traits of the anima of Apuleius-Lucius: his passionate longing for knowledge (*curiositas*) and his inclination toward magic, whose purpose is to manipulate the divine forces instead of serving them," p. 108.

Chapter 6

1. In discussing "Old Greek Alchemy," von Franz refers to "the Old Greek text which is in the Codex Marcianus. It probably belongs to what we call the oldest writings and is entitled 'The Prophetess Isis to her Son.' . . . The document probably goes back to about the 1st century A.D. . . . It might be older . . . Certainly based on older texts . . . " She goes on to point out that, in early texts, there are references to "The holy technique" that was part of initiation. "'The holy technique'—*hiera techne*—refers to alchemy." Marie-Louise von Franz, *Alchemy: An Introduction to the Symbolism and the Psychology* (Toronto: Inner City Books, 1980), pp. 43–44.

2. According to C. C. Zain in *Spiritual Alchemy: The Hermetic Art of Spiritual Transformation,* "the word Alchemy . . . is Arabic, being derived from *al,* the, and *kimia,* hidden . . . To the Arabians alchemy was the science of hidden properties and essences." (Los Angeles: Church of Light, 1995), p. 2. David Goddard in *The Tower of Alchemy: An Advanced Guide to the Great Work,* says: "'Alchemy' is the Arabic word for 'the Matter of Egypt,' derived from the ancient name for the land of the Nile valley, *Khem,* meaning the Black Land" (York Beach, MF.: Weiser, 1999), p. 1.

3. The Hellenistic Egyptian Hermes was believed to be the son of Thoth—the first scribe and god of all learning, language, and hidden wisdom. Thoth was called the "Revealer of the Hidden" and "Lord of Rebirth" and the initiator of human enlightenment and wisdom. "Thoth presides over the 'Weighing of the Heart' ceremony, which determines who is admitted into heaven," observes Dennis William Hauck, *The Emerald Tablet: Alchemy for Personal Transformation* (New York: Penguin Arkana, 1999), p. 24. In the story one of his forms is Zeus. He was also equated at times with Osiris. Jewish mystics often identify Thoth with Seth, the second son of Adam. For them Enoch, whose name means "the initiated," is an angelic being who was described in much the same way as Thoth and Hermes. According to the texts used by von Franz, "the secret of alchemy (was handed over) by the angel Amnaël to the goddess Isis," von Franz, *Alchemy,* p. 65.

4. See Lyndy Abraham, *A Dictionary of Alchemical Imagery* (Cambridge, UK: Cambridge University Press, 1998); Hauck, *The Emerald Tablet.*

Chapter 7

1. "According to the scholastic theory of knowledge, you can only get knowledge through love, which means that you only acquire knowledge by loving your subject, by being fascinated by it." Marie-Louise von Franz, *Alchemy: An Introduction to the Symbolism and the Psychology* (Toronto: Inner City Books, 1980), p. 116.

Chapter 8

1. Von Franz suggests that "the search for immortality was actually the search for an incorruptible essence in man which would survive death, an essential part of the human being which could be preserved . . . (And this) search . . . is to be found at the very beginning of alchemy." Marie-Louise von Franz, *Alchemy: An Introduction to the Symbolism and the Psychology* (Toronto: Inner City Books, 1980), pp. 93–94.

Chapter 9

1. See Plato, *The Collected Dialogues of Plato Including The Letters*, Edith Hamilton and Huntington Cairns, eds. (New York: Pantheon, 1961); *Plato: Complete Works,* edited with introduction and notes by John M. Cooper (Indianapolis, IN: Hackett Publishing, 1997); *Plato's Thought*, edited and translated by G.M.A. Grube (Boston: Beacon Press, 1958); and *The Basic Works of Aristotle*, Richard McKeon, trans. (New York: Random House, 1941).

2. Dennis William Hauck, *The Emerald Tablet: Alchemy for Personal Transformation* (London: Penguin Arkana, 1999), p. 64.

3. Hauck, *The Emerald Tablet*, p. 65.

4. Hauck, *The Emerald Tablet*, p. 72.

5. Marie-Louise von Franz elaborates on the nigredo in *Alchemy: An Introduction to the Symbolism and the Psychology* (Toronto: Inner City Books, 1980): "The black cloud is a well-known alchemical symbol for the state called the *nigredo*, the blackness which very often occurs first in the opus; if you distill the material it evaporates and for a while you see nothing but a kind of confusion or cloud, which the alchemist compared to the earth being covered up by a black cloud . . . 'The Cloud of Unknowing,' a mystical medieval text . . . describes the fact that the closer the soul of the mystic gets to the Godhead the darker and more confused he becomes. Such texts say in effect that God lives in the cloud of unknowing and that one has to be stripped of every idea, every intellectual conception, before one can approach the light which is surrounded by the darkness of utter confusion" (p. 208); and "In alchemical literature it is generally said that the great effort and trouble continues from the *nigredo* to the *albedo*; that is said to be the hard part, and afterwards everything becomes easier. The *nigredo*—the blackness, the terrible depression and state of dissolution—has to be compensated by the hard work of the alchemist and that hard work consists, among other things, in constant washing . . ." (p. 220).

6. Lyndy Abraham, *A Dictionary of Alchemical Imagery* (Cambridge, UK: Cambridge University Press, 1998), p. 51.

7. Hauck, *The Emerald Tablet*, p. 101.

Chapter 10

1. A very different interpretation is given by von Franz: "the negative sisters who ruin Psyche are both unhappily married, having married for money and power, and they obviously represent a destructive side of the power complex, which destroys every true feeling relationship. They symbolize the greedy, envious force, the jealousy, possessiveness, and miserliness of the soul which does not want to give itself to an inner or outer love experience, together with the inability to get away from the banal aspect of life." *The Golden Ass of Apuleius* (Boston: Shambhala, 1992), pp. 98–99. C. S. Lewis gives an entirely different view of the sisters in his novel *Till We Have Faces* (New York: Harcourt Brace Jovanovich, 1980).

Chapter 11

1. According to von Franz, in some Greek stories the ant extracts gold from the earth. She

also relates that Karl Kerényi points out that in one Greek myth the original inhabitants of the earth were ant-people, "Myrmekanthropoi." Marie-Louise von Franz, *The Golden Ass of Apuleius* (Boston: Shambhala, 1992).

2. In ancient Egypt, the hieroglyph for "reed" represented Horus, the reborn sun god, as well as the king of Egypt.

3. In ancient Egypt, the ram was closely associated with the goddess Isis and thus is a reference to both Aphrodite (the Greek form of Isis) and to the end of the larger novel when Lucius is initiated into the cult of Isis.

4. This is also a reference to the Nile as a river of life and death.

Chapter 12

1. See Martin Lowenthal, *Dawning of Clear Light* (Charlottesville, VA: Hampton Roads, 2003).

2. See Peter Kingsley, *In the Dark Places of Wisdom* (Inverness, CA: The Golden Sufi Center, 1999).

3. This is the view in many traditions besides the ancient Greek. The *Rig Veda* of India says that "in the beginning darkness existed, enveloped in darkness." For the Marquesas Islanders, the beginning was boundless night, *Po*, that which included everything and was ruled by *Tanaoa*, which means "darkness," and *Mutu-hei*, which means "silence."

Chapter 13

1. In the biblical myth of Adam and Eve, according to a Kabbalistic description, God officiated at their wedding and all of creation was gathered to participate in the celebration.

2. Lyndy Abraham, *A Dictionary of Alchemical Imagery* (Cambridge, UK: Cambridge University Press, 1998), p. 145.

3. Martín Prechtel, *The Disobedience of the Daughter of the Sun* (Cambridge, MA: Yellow Moon Press, 2001), p. 121.

SELECTED BIBLIOGRAPHY

Translations of Apuleius

Adlington, William, ed. and trans. in 1566 and revised by S. Gaselee in 1915. *The Golden Ass of Apuleius*. Cambridge: Harvard University Press, 1915.

Butler, H. E., trans. *The Metamorphoses or Golden Ass of Apuleius of Madaura*. Oxford: Clarendon Press, 1910.

Graves, Robert, trans. *The Golden Ass of Apuleius*. New York: Farrar, Straus and Young, 1951.

Hanson, J. Arthur, ed. and trans. *Metamorphoses*. Cambridge: Harvard University Press, 1989.

Kenney, E. J., ed. *Cupid and Psyche*. Cambridge, UK: Cambridge University Press, 1990.

————, trans. With introduction and notes. *The Golden Ass or Metamorphoses*. London: Penguin Classics, 1998.

Other Sources

Aristophanes. *Ten Greek Plays*. Gilbert Murray, J. H. Frere, and D. K. Sandford, trans., Gilbert Murray ed. New York: Oxford University Press, 1929.

Aristotle. *The Basic Works of Aristotle*. Richard McKeon, trans. New York: Random House, 1941.

Bachelard, Gaston. *The Poetics of Reverie*. Boston: Beacon Press, 1969.

Bak, Samuel. *Painted in Words: A Memoir*. Bloomington, IN: Indiana University Press, 2001.

Barry, Kieren. *The Greek Qabalah*. York Beach, ME: Samuel Weiser, 1999.

Bernouli, Rudolf. "Spiritual Development as Reflected in Alchemy and Related Disciplines," in *Spiritual Disciplines,* Joseph Campbell, ed. Princeton, NJ: Princeton University Press, 1960.

Binder, G. and R. Merkelbach, eds. "Amor und Psyche" in *Wege der Forchung,* Vol. 126. Darmstadt, Germany: Wissenschaftliche Buchgesellschaft, 1968.

Bowra, C. M. *The Greek Experience.* New York: Mentor Books, 1957.

Campbell, Joseph. *The Masks of God: Occidental Mythology.* New York: Penguin Books, 1964.

———. *The Mythic Image.* Princeton, NJ: Princeton University Press, 1974.

———. *The Power of Myth.* New York: Doubleday, 1988.

Edinger, Edward. *Anatomy of the Psyche: Alchemical Symbolism in Psychotherapy.* LaSalle, IL: Open Court Publishing, 1985.

Eliade, Mircea. *Rites and Symbols of Initiation: The Mysteries of Birth and Rebirth.* Willard Trask, trans. New York: Harper and Row, 1965.

Estés, Clarissa Pinkola. *Women Who Run With the Wolves.* New York: Ballantine, 1992.

Fromm, Eric. *The Forgotten Language: An Introduction to the Understanding of Dreams, Fairy Tales, and Myths.* New York: Grove Press, 1951.

Gafni, Marc. *Soul Prints: Your Path to Fulfillment.* New York: Simon and Schuster, 2001.

Gilchrist, Cherry. *The Elements of Alchemy.* Rockport, MA: Element Books, 1991.

Gilligan, Carol. *The Birth of Pleasure.* New York: Alfred A. Knopf, 2002.

Goddard, David. *The Tower of Alchemy: An Advanced Guide to the Great Work.* York Beach, ME: Samuel Weiser, 1999.

Gollnick, James. *Love and the Soul: Psychological Interpretations of the Eros and Psyche Myth*. Waterloo, Ontario: Wilfrid Laurier University Press, 1992.

Goodrich, Norma Lorre. *The Ancient Myths*. New York: Mentor Books, 1960.

Graves, Robert. *The Greek Myths, Volume One*. New York: George Braziller, 1959.

Hauck, Dennis William. *The Emerald Tablet: Alchemy for Personal Transformation*. New York: Penguin Arkana, 1999.

Hesiod. *Theogony, Works, and Days*. M. L. West, ed. and trans. Oxford, England: Oxford University Press, 1988.

Hillman, James. *Insearch: Psychology and Religion*. Irving,TX: Spring Publications, 1979.

Homer. *The Iliad*. Samuel Butler, trans. Roslyn, NY: Walter J. Black, 1942.

———. *The Odyssey*. Samuel Butler, trans. Roslyn, NY: Walter J. Black, 1944.

Houston, Jean. *The Search for The Beloved: Journeys in Sacred Psychology*. Los Angeles, CA: J. P. Tarcher, 1987.

James, Paula. *Unity in diversity: a study of Apuleius' "Metamorphoses": with particular reference to the narrator's art of transformation and the metamorphosis motif in the Tale of Cupid and Psyche*. Hildesheim, Germany: Olms-Weimann, 1987.

Johnson, Robert A. *She: Understanding Feminine Psychology*. New York: Harper and Row, 1977.

Jung, C. G. *The Basic Writings of C. G. Jung*. Ed. with introduction by Violet Staub de Laszlo. New York: Modern Library, 1959.

———. *The Portable Jung*. Joseph Campbell, ed. New York: Penguin, 1976.

———. *Psyche and Symbol: A Selection of Writings of C. G. Jung*. Violet Staub de Laszlo, ed. Garden City, NJ: Doubleday Anchor, 1958.

———. *Psychology and the East*. R.F.C. Hull, trans. Princeton, NJ: Princeton University Press, 1978.

Jung, C. G., ed. *Man and His Symbols*. New York: Dell, 1968.

Kingsley, Peter. *In the Dark Places of Wisdom*. Inverness, CA: The Golden Sufi Center, 1999.

Lewis, C. S. *Till We Have Faces*. New York: Harcourt Brace Jovanovich, 1980.

Lindsay, Jack. *The Origins of Alchemy in Greco-Roman Egypt*. Oxford, England: Oxford University Press, 1970.

Lockhart, Russell. *Words as Eggs: Psyche in Language and Clinic*. Dallas, TX: Spring Publications, 1983.

Lowenthal, Martin. *Dawning of Clear Light*. Charlottesville, VA: Hampton Roads, 2003.

Mathews, Caitlin and John. *The Western Way: A Practical Guide to the Western Mystery Tradition*. New York: Penguin Arkana, 1994.

Mead, G. R. S. *Thrice Greatest Hermes: Studies in Hellenistic Theosophy and Gnosis*. York Beach, ME: Samuel Weiser, 1992.

Miller, Richard and Iona. *The Modern Alchemist: A Guide to Personal Transformation*. Grand Rapids, MI: Phanes Press, 1994.

Neumann, Erich. *Amor and Psyche: The Psychic Development of the Feminine*. Ralph Mannheim, trans. Princeton, NJ: Princeton University Press, 1965.

Odier, Daniel. *Desire: The Tantric Path to Awakening*. Rochester, VT: Inner Traditions, 2001.

Pater, Walter. *The Marriage of Cupid and Psyche*. New York: Heritage Press, 1951.

Pernety, Antoine-Joseph. *An Alchemical Treatise on the Great Art: A System of Physics According to the Hermetic Philosophy*. York Beach, ME: Samuel Weiser, 1995.

Plato. *The Collected Dialogues of Plato Including The Letters*. Edith Hamilton and Huntington Cairns, eds. New York: Pantheon, 1961.

———. *Plato: Complete Works.* Ed. with introduction and notes by John M. Cooper. Indianapolis, IN: Hackett Publishing, 1997.

———. *Plato's Thought.* Ed. and trans. by G. M. A. Grube. Boston: Beacon Press, 1958.

Prechtel, Martín. *The Disobedience of the Daughter of the Sun.* Cambridge, MA: Yellow Moon Press, 2001.

Ramsay, Jay. *Alchemy: The Art of Transformation.* San Francisco: HarperCollins Thorsons, 1997.

Salaman, Clement and Dorine van Oyen, William D. Wharton, Jean-Pierre Mahé. *The Way of Hermes: New Translations of The Corpus Hermeticum and The Definitions of Hermes Trismegistus to Asclepius.* Rochester, VT: Inner Traditions, 2000.

Small, Jacquelyn, *Psyche's Seeds.* New York: J. P. Tarcher/Putnam, 2001.

von Franz, Marie-Louise. *Alchemical Active Imagination.* Irving, TX: Spring Publications, 1979.

———. *Alchemy: An Introduction to the Symbolism and the Psychology.* Toronto: Inner City Books, 1980.

———. *The Golden Ass of Apuleius: The Liberation of the Feminine in Man.* Boston: Shambhala, 1992.

Zain, C. C. *Spiritual Alchemy: The Hermetic Art of Spiritual Transformation.* Los Angeles: Church of Light, 1995.

Reference Dictionaries

Abraham, Lyndy. *A Dictionary of Alchemical Imagery.* Cambridge, UK: Cambridge University Press, 1998.

American Heritage Dictionary of the English Language. Boston: Houghton Mifflin, 1969.

Cirlot, J. E. *A Dictionary of Symbols.* Trans. Jack Sage, foreword by Herbert Read. New York: Philosophical Library, 1962.

Cotterell, Arthur. *A Dictionary of World Mythology.* New York: Putnam, 1979.

de Vries, Ad. *Dictionary of Symbols and Imagery.* Amsterdam: North-Holland Publishing, 1974.

Drury, Nevill. *Dictionary of Mysticism and the Esoteric Traditions.* Dorset, UK: Prism Press, 1992.

Gaskell, G. A. *Dictionary of Scripture and Myth.* New York: Dorset Press, 1988.

Grimal, Pierre. *The Dictionary of Classical Mythology.* A. R. Maxwell-Hyslop, trans. Oxford, England: Blackwell Publishers, 1986.

Haeffner, Mark. *Dictionary of Alchemy.* San Francisco, CA: HarperCollins Aquarian, 1994.

Walker, Barbara G. *The Women's Encyclopedia of Myths and Secrets.* New York: Harper and Row, 1983.

INDEX

ABOUT THE AUTHOR

MARTIN LOWENTHAL, PH.D. is an ordained senior meditation teacher and mentor with the Dedicated Life Institute. Dr. Lowenthal is the author of *Dawning of Clear Light*, *Embrace Yes*, and co-author of *Opening the Heart of Compassion*. In addition to conducting workshops and retreats internationally, he serves as a pastoral counselor, consultant, and writer. He has been on the faculty of Boston College and Harvard University Extension and has studied with Buddhist and Taoist masters for more than thirty years. Dr. Lowenthal received his doctorate from the University of California, Berkeley in 1970, has worked as an applied anthropologist in Botswana, Africa, and directed a research institute from 1970 to 1977. A practicing psychotherapist, he lives with his wife Karen in Newton, Massachusetts.

DEDICATED LIFE INSTITUTE

Cultivating Wisdom Presence for Everyday Life

THE DEDICATED LIFE INSTITUTE (DLI) supports spiritual exploration and growth and is dedicated to making the essence teachings of many traditions accessible in a Western idiom. Incorporating the principles of the mystic way, we promote both recovery of our wisdom ground of being and development of our capacity to use our daily conditions as a means of growth and the opportunity to manifest our true wisdom nature. Our dedication to living as an expression of wisdom serves to encourage both personal and social transformation. Founded by Martin Lowenthal, the Institute offers meditation groups, retreats, workshops, and a home study program. For more information please contact:

> Dedicated Life Institute
> 53 Westchester Road
> Newton, Massachusetts 02458
> Phone: 617-527-8606
> Visit our web site: www.dli.org
> e-mail: mldli@rcn.org